Lead People

Build Trust, Teams, and
Transformational Culture

Dennis Ducatt

Lead People: Build Trust, Teams, and Transformational Culture

© 2025 by Dennis Ducatt
All Rights Reserved
Published by Ingram Spark

All rights reserved. No part of this book may be reproduced in any form or by any means - electronic, mechanical, photocopying, scanning, or otherwise - without written permission in writing from the publisher, except by a reviewer who may quote brief passages in a review.

Paperback ISBN: 979-8-9937087-0-6

Printed in the United States of America

Table of Contents

Introduction	4
PART I: EXEMPLIFY	7
Chapter 1: The Leader as Creator - Vision, Mission, and Culture	8
Chapter 2: Exemplify Skills - Mastering the Essential Competencies	20
Chapter 3: Exemplify Skills - Mastering the Essential Competencies	32
Chapter 4: Leading by Example - Modeling at Every Level	49
PART II: STRATEGIZE	
Chapter 5: Researching and Evaluating Your Business Environment	66
Chapter 6: Writing Your Strategic Plan	93
Chapter 7: Executing Your Strategic Plan	112
PART III: COMMUNICATE	125
Chapter 8: Mastering Leadership Communication	126
Chapter 9: Understanding and Engaging Your Followers	140
Chapter 10: Conversation and Persuasion	151
PART IV: MOTIVATE	164
Chapter 11: Recruiting and Building Your Team	165

Introduction

Let me pose a question to you: How many leadership books have you read that got you pumped up for a week or so, only to have reality kick in, and you were once again stuck dealing with the same old problems?

If you are like most leaders, the answer is likely "too many to count." The leadership development field is replete with theories, models, and motivational speeches that often fail to translate into the daily realities of what it actually takes to lead real people with real problems.

The issue is not that you are not doing enough or that you are not sufficiently good. The problem is that the majority of leadership guidance addresses symptoms, not the actual issue: what leadership is and how it works in practice.

So let us start with clarity.

Leadership is the enlightened inspiration of followers to achieve exceptional results. Observe what this definition does not state—it's not a matter of being the most intelligent person in the room, knowing all the answers, or telling people what to do through fiat. It's a matter of inspiring people, and doing so in an enlightened way that leads to results beyond expectations.

Suppose you've been finding it difficult to obtain consistent performance from your team, finding yourself working harder than everyone else on the team, or questioning why some leaders can motivate so effortlessly while you're grinding away like you're trying to push a boulder uphill. If that's you, this book is what you have been waiting for.

This book is a practical how-to guide—a blueprint for what effective leaders actually do. Through my work with leaders at every level, from front-line managers to C-suite executives, I've identified a clear pattern in how successful leaders operate. They may not even realize it, but they instinctively focus their efforts on what I call the On Target Leadership Framework.

This is not another theoretical model designed solely to impress on PowerPoint slides. This is a practical framework based on four areas where effective leaders concentrate their daily efforts:

- Exemplify - This is about who you are as a leader: your character, your ability, and the example you set daily. People will follow leaders they respect, and respect is founded on a consistent showing of character and ability.

- Strategize - This is where you're going and how you're going to get there. It's an honest acknowledgment of where you are now, developing a plausible plan, and disciplining yourself to follow through and be accountable.

- Communicate - This is how you deal with people. It is not just about being a good speaker—it is about being capable of reading people, being understood, and persuading people to come along with you.

- Motivate - This involves getting the best from your people. It begins with recruiting the right people, continues through constant motivation and direction, and encompasses praising and rewarding quality where you see it.

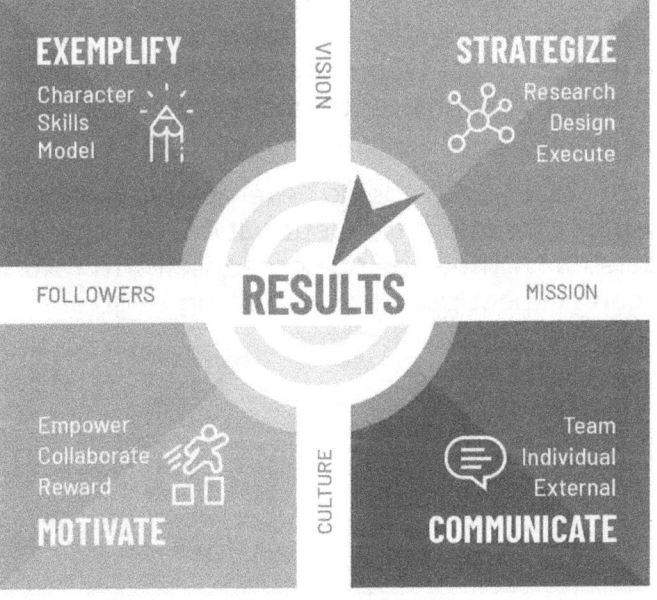

Each of these four areas has three specific components that we'll explore in detail throughout this book. Here's what's crucial to understand: these four areas don't operate in isolation. They work together within your organization's vision, mission, and culture to create a leadership approach that is authentic to you and actually gets results.

You'll notice this book is practical. Each concept has specific strategies you can apply immediately. Each chapter concludes with action steps. This is not about adding more theory to your leadership toolbox—it's about providing you with a tested system that works in the real world.

By the time you finish this book, you'll not only understand what good leadership looks like, but you'll know how to practice it every day. You'll learn how to be the kind of leader that makes people want to follow you, how to develop and execute strategic plans that actually work, how to communicate in ways that genuinely connect with people, and how to motivate your team to achieve things they never thought possible.

We start with being exemplary leaders and building character, the foundation of all effective leadership. Without being someone worth following, you can't expect people to be willing to go anywhere with you.

Let's go!

Introduction

PART I: EXEMPLIFY
Who You Are as a Leader

Chapter 1

The Leader as Creator - Vision, Mission, and Culture

You've likely read a couple of dozen leadership books by this point. You may have attended numerous seminars, listened to motivational speakers, and gathered business cards at networking meetings. And yet here you are, still looking for something that translates to the real world of leading people.

Here's what most leadership advice gets wrong: it approaches leadership as management with good communication skills. Leadership, however, is not about managing what already is—it's about developing what is not yet. Throughout history, the narrative of humanity has been propelled by individuals who dared to envision a world beyond the one they were given. You, as a leader, are not a manager of what is, but the designer of what could be—a creator of the future.

The Essence of Leadership: Beyond Management

Whereas a manager might battle everyday realities, you, as a leader, need to develop a special relationship with the future, not as an event to be waited for, but as a landscape to be discovered and crafted. The future is never received passively; acts of courage, tenacity, and resilience create it.

Look at it pragmatically. Daily, you are confronted with issues that lack definable solutions, teams that must be led to goals that have never been met before, and problems that call for you to envision a reality other than the one you are presently experiencing. You are not merely overseeing today's work—you are building tomorrow's potential.

Reflection Question

Think about a recent challenge you faced as a leader. Were you managing the problem as it existed, or were you creating a solution that didn't exist before? What was the difference in your approach?

Leaders, both renowned and unsung, make lasting impressions in their communities, organizations, countries, and even the world at large through their ability to envision and implement new realities. To create is what you do in three basic ways that are the building blocks of all you'll be doing as a leader:

- You generate vision - You envision possibilities others cannot see yet, and you render those possibilities tangible and persuasive to your team.
- You create a mission - You establish why the work is essential and provide individuals with a reason to dedicate their energy and talent.
- You build culture - you influence the way individuals think, behave, and interact with one another in pursuit of common objectives.

Vision: The Spark That Ignites the Future

At the root of effective leadership is vision—the capacity to look beyond the current conditions and envision new horizons of possibility. Vision, in its strongest form, is not some esoteric ideal but a real force that inspires action and consolidates collective effort. Excellent leaders perceive potential where others perceive limitations. They create a sense of purpose that emanates outward, touching all those with whom they come into contact.

Take, for example, the reinvention of Apple Inc. through the visionary leadership of Steve Jobs. When Jobs rejoined an ailing Apple in the late 1990s, its prospects were in doubt (Isaacson, 2012). By challenging himself to imagine a world where technology was not just powerful but also elegant and user-friendly, Jobs paved the way for revolutionary innovations such as the iPod, iPhone, and iPad. His vision galvanized a team and, in fact, an entire industry to reimagine the intersection of humans and technology.

This capacity to envision beyond the status quo is not unique to business leaders. In politics, Franklin D. Roosevelt's New Deal emerged during the depths of the Great Depression (Library of Congress, n.d.). Roosevelt's vision of a country rejuvenated through public works projects and social programs reshaped American society and established a model for activist government in the face of crisis. His fireside chats, which were optimistic in tone, helped to galvanize the American public around a shared sense of hope and resolve.

Vision is also apparent in the scientific world. Marie Curie, the trailblazing physicist, was dissatisfied with the limits of established science. Through her work in radioactivity, a phenomenon that was then shrouded in mystery, she broke new ground, essentially changing our understanding of matter and energy (Fröman, 1996). There is a lesson in Curie's work for all leaders: to build the future, one must challenge, search, and at times navigate through the darkness propelled by the glow of curiosity and conviction alone.

The Anatomy of Effective Vision

But vision, however bold, needs to be grounded in reality. The best leaders don't ignore current limitations; instead, they engage in profound observation and analysis to spot seeds of possibility in the current circumstances. Here is what you have to master:

- Imagination - The creative jump that enables you to visualize what others do not. This is not daydreaming but focused thinking on possibilities that may arise from present realities.

- Clarity - Being able to communicate the vision in a manner that is comprehensible and inspiring to others. If you cannot explain it simply, you do not know it well enough to lead by it.

- Groundedness - The self-control to anchor vision in reality so that it is attainable instead of unrealistic. Your vision must challenge people, not crush them.

- Commitment - The resolve to follow the vision relentlessly, even when confronted by hurdles. Vision without commitment is mere daydreaming.

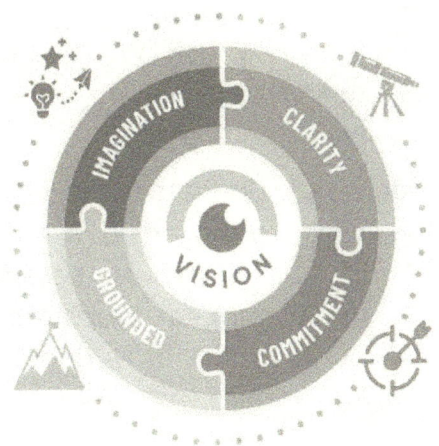

Making Vision Practical

Here is how to create and share a vision that really works:
1. Begin with profound observation.
    - Take time to actually observe what's going on in your organization, your industry, your team.
    - What's working? What's not? What possibilities are buried in current problems?

2. Ask transformational questions.
    - Rather than "How do we repair this problem?" ask "What would success look like if we completely solved this?"
    - Rather than "Why is this not working?" ask "What would we need to shift to make this work better than we ever imagined?"
3. Unite seemingly unrelated elements.
    - Vision often arises from connecting ideas, trends, or possibilities that initially appear unrelated. Search for patterns others overlook.
4. Make it real.
    - The most effective visions are not general inspirational pronouncements. They are concrete images of what the future will be like, feel like, and provide to actual human beings.

Practical Activity: Vision Development Exercise

Current State Analysis (15 minutes)

- List 5 significant challenges your team/organization currently faces
- Identify three opportunities that exist within these challenges
- Note any trends or patterns you observe

Future State Imagination (20 minutes)

- For each opportunity, write a brief description of what success would look like in 2-3 years.
- Ask yourself: "If we solved this completely, what would be different?"
- Make it specific: What would people be doing? How would they feel? What results would we see?

Vision Statement Draft (10 minutes)

- Combine your future state descriptions into 2-3 sentences
- Test it: Can you explain this vision to someone in under 30 seconds?
- Refine until it's both inspiring and concrete.

Vision is the spark that sets the future ablaze. Vision is not a snapshot but a living entity, continuously sharpened through dialogue, feedback, and reflection.

Mission: The Bridge to Meaningful Work

With vision informing individuals of direction, mission informs each person why it's a trip worth taking and provides significance to their everyday tasks.

Your mission is not your firm's mission statement—although they ought to coincide. Your mission is the particular reason why the work of your team is significant in the larger scheme.

It's the response to the question each individual on your team is wondering: "Why should I care about this beyond my salary?"

Mission converts individual tasks into a shared purpose. When individuals know not only what they're doing but also why it counts, their involvement and performance improve dramatically. This is not theoretical—it's quantifiable in productivity, retention, and innovation.

Developing An Inspirational Mission

An inspirational mission should link everyday work to significant results. It helps people understand how their individual tasks contribute to something greater. If you are managing a customer service group, the purpose is not "answer calls quickly." It is "solve problems that make people's lives easier" or "turn frustrated customers into loyal advocates."

So, be specific about impact. Vague missions, such as "excellence" or "innovation," don't motivate anyone. Specific missions like "reduce patient wait times by 50% so families spend less time worrying and more time healing" give people something concrete to work toward.

Also, make it personal. The most effective missions tie into what your team members already care about. Take the time to learn what drives each individual, then connect the team's mission to their individual goals and values.

> **Interactive Exercise: Mission Clarity Check**
>
> Rate your current team's mission on a scale of 1-10 for each category:
>
> - Clarity: Can everyone on your team explain the mission in their own words? ___/10
> - Connection: Do team members understand how their daily tasks contribute to the mission? ___/10
> - Inspiration: Does the mission energize people and make them want to do their best work? ___/10
> - Measurement: Can you track progress toward fulfilling the mission? ___/10
>
> Total Score: ___/40
>
> - 32-40: Your mission is strong and motivating
> - 24-31: Good foundation, but could be more compelling
> - 16-23: Mission exists, but isn't driving behavior
> - Below 16: Time to rebuild your mission from the ground up

Then, be sure to link it to a larger purpose. Illustrate how your team's purpose contributes to the organization's overall mission and ultimately leads to something significant in the world.

Culture: The Operating System of Your Team

Culture is where mission and vision meet in everyday interaction. It's the set of habits, attitudes, and behaviors that define how work really happens when you're not looking. Culture is the operating system that either fuels or derails everything else you're attempting to do.

Most executives believe that culture develops organically. It's like assuming software creates itself. Hundreds of tiny, deliberate decisions you make daily establish an organization's culture.

The Elements of Cultural Creation

- Psychological Safety - A climate where people feel comfortable taking risks without fear of reprisal. Individuals must think they can speak up, make errors, and question ideas without punishment.

- Diversity of Thought - The presence of different viewpoints, backgrounds, and experiences to facilitate creativity. Homogeneous thinking yields predictable outcomes.

- Resource Allocation - The way time, money, and resources are allocated reveals what is truly valued, regardless of what is communicated.

- Leadership Support - Champions who believe in the mission and eliminate barriers to its execution.

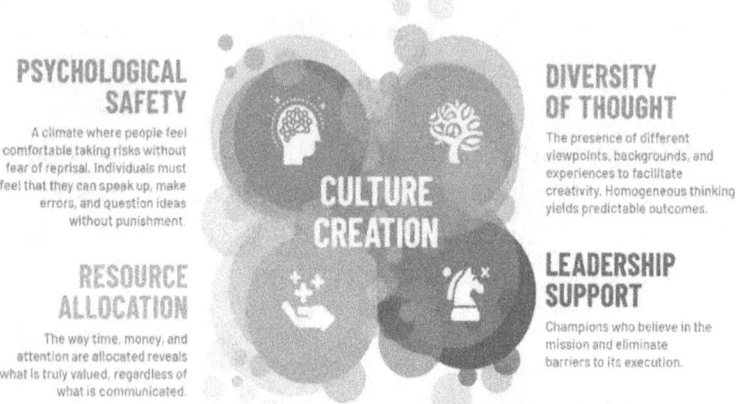

Building Culture Intentionally

Model the behavior you wish to see. If you desire a culture of accountability, be accountable. If you expect innovation, try new things publicly and praise smart failures. If you want collaboration, collaborate—do not simply delegate.

Create systems that support values. At Google, the culture supports experimentation and accepts failure since their systems—from hiring to performance reviews to project funding—all reward iteration and learning (Grossman, 2024). Toyota's dedication to "kaizen," or continuous improvement, empowers employees at all levels to suggest improvements and enhance systems (Toyota Blog, 2013). This innovation culture is not an accident; it is a result of intentional leadership decisions.

Fix problems promptly. Nothing kills culture more quickly than accepting behavior that is counter to your professed values. If you claim to value respect but permit disrespectful behavior to persist, you've just informed everyone that your values are optional, not obligatory.

Reward the correct behaviors. What is rewarded gets repeated. Ensure your reward and recognition systems support the culture you are attempting to build.

Practical Activity: Culture Audit

Step 1: Identify Your Intended Culture (10 minutes)
- Write down 3-5 values or behaviors you want to characterize your team's culture.
- Examples: collaboration, innovation, accountability, customer focus, continuous learning

Step 2: Audit Your Current Practices (15 minutes)
For each intended value, ask:
- What do you currently measure that reinforces this value?
- What do you currently reward that reinforces this value?
- What do you currently celebrate that reinforces this value?
- What behaviors do you tolerate that contradict this value?

Step 3: Identify Gaps (10 minutes)
- Where are your systems not aligned with your intended culture?
- What behaviors are you accidentally rewarding that you don't want?
- What positive behaviors go unrecognized?

Step 4: Create Action Steps (15 minutes)
- Choose 2-3 specific changes you can make this month

- Identify what you'll start doing, stop doing, or do differently
- Set a follow-up date to reassess progress

Courage: The Bridge between Vision and Reality

Vision, mission, and a strong culture remain inert without the courage to pursue them. The future is never passively received; it is forged through acts of daring, persistence, and resilience. Courage is what empowers you to take that first step into the unknown, often in the face of skepticism, resistance, or outright hostility.

Consider Rosa Parks, whose quiet refusal to surrender her seat on a segregated bus sparked a movement that transformed American civil rights. The bravery of Parks was not only in her defiance, but in her readiness to suffer for the sake of a cause larger than herself.

In business, courage can take the form of making a risky change of direction at a pivotal moment. When Netflix co-founder Reed Hastings made the switch from renting DVDs by mail to streaming video with no proven model, the decision was fraught with peril (Hibler, 2025). However, Hastings' bravery in forging ahead into the unknown ultimately transformed the entertainment business.

The Dimensions of Leadership Courage

- Physical Courage - The courage to encounter danger or adversity when required.
- Moral Courage - The willingness to stand for principles and ethics, even if unpopular or at a price.
- Intellectual Courage - The willingness to question your own beliefs and to consider new ideas that may challenge comfortable assumptions.
- Emotional Courage - The ability to be vulnerable, to own up to mistakes, and to ask for help when necessary.

Reflection Questions

- When have you demonstrated each type of courage in your leadership role?
- Which type of courage do you find most challenging to exercise?
- What would you do differently in your current role if you had unlimited courage?

Innovation: The Driver of Creativity

Innovation is the pragmatic engine that powers the construction of the future. Though courage accelerates action, it is through innovation that novel solutions, systems, and paradigms emerge. Innovative leaders promote change, defy orthodoxies, and develop cultures in which experimentation is not merely acceptable but expected.

The tale of human progress is, at its core, the story of innovation. Katherine Johnson, whose math helped launch astronauts into space, reminds us that breakthroughs occur when people are empowered to apply their unique set of skills to new problems (Toole, 2020). Likewise, Tim Berners-Lee's development of the World Wide Web has revolutionized nearly every facet of contemporary existence.

Social innovators like Muhammad Yunus, who founded Grameen Bank, have redesigned financial systems to benefit the world's poorest populations, introducing microfinance and promoting economic empowerment (Liberto, 2022). Their innovative leadership demonstrates that innovation can address profound social issues.

Interactive Exercise: Innovation Opportunity Mapping

Part A: Identify Innovation Zones (20 minutes)
- List your team's top three recurring problems or inefficiencies
- Identify two processes that haven't changed in over a year
- Note one customer/stakeholder complaint you hear regularly

Part B: Apply Innovation Thinking (20 minutes)
For each item above, ask:
- "What if we could eliminate this problem rather than just manage it?"
- "What would this look like if we designed it from scratch today?"
- "How do successful organizations in other industries handle similar challenges?"

Part C: Generate Experiments (15 minutes)
- Choose your most promising innovation opportunity.
- Design a small, low-risk experiment you could run in the next 30 days
- Identify what you'll measure to determine if the experiment worked
- Plan how you'll involve your team in the innovation process

The Framework in Action

As mentioned in the introduction to this book, we will discuss how successful leaders apply this creator role in four key areas that constitute the complete leadership model: exemplifying, strategizing, communicating, and motivating.

The final test of your success as a leader and innovator lies not in your short-term achievements, but in your legacy. Legacy represents the summation of vision, courage, innovation, inspiration, structure, and adaptability—the lasting impact of your leadership on individuals, processes, institutions, and the world at large.

Nelson Mandela dedicated himself to reconciliation over revenge, working to heal a torn nation (Pollitt, 2013). Ruth Bader Ginsburg, whose legal work over the decades advanced gender equality, galvanized generations of activists and legislators (Rao, 2025). These leaders sow seeds whose harvest comes long after their own participation has ceased.

Legacy is not the sole domain of the powerful or well-known. Teachers, mentors, and community leaders create the future daily through the people they touch and the values they teach. Their actions send out ripples that affect families, neighborhoods, and societies in ways that may never be fully understood or quantified.

Building Your Legacy as a Creator

- Mentorship - Invest time and effort in grooming future leaders.

- Transmission of Values - Incorporate fundamental values into organizational culture and daily practice.

- Sustainable Innovation - Develop systems that encourage continuous creativity and adaptation.

- Community Impact - Engage with broader societal issues and contribute to the public good.

> **Personal Leadership Commitment Exercise**
>
> Step 1: Legacy Vision (15 minutes)
> - Write a brief description of how you want to be remembered as a leader
> - What impact do you want to have on the people you lead?
> - What changes do you want to create that will outlast your current role?
>
> Step 2: Current Reality Check (10 minutes)
> - What are you doing now that moves you toward that legacy?
> - What are you doing that might undermine it?
> - What's missing from your current approach?
>
> Step 3: Next Steps (10 minutes)
> - Identify three specific actions you can take in the next 90 days
> - Choose one behavior you'll start, one you'll stop, and one you'll modify
> - Set calendar reminders to review your progress monthly

Wrapping It Up

Keep in mind, this is not a matter of being a visionary genius or charismatic inspiration. It's a matter of being deliberate and disciplined about doing your basic job as a leader: building a future that does not yet exist.

You accomplish this by:
- Seeing possibilities others miss through disciplined observation and imagination
- Making those possibilities attractive and attainable by communicating clearly
- Developing systems and cultures that translate vision into reality through habitual action
- Encouraging others to follow you in creation work through genuine leadership

Each challenge you confront as a leader is a chance to create. Each problem is raw material for making something better. Each day, you can envision a different reality and take practical steps to bring it into being.

To lead is to create—to dream boldly, act decisively, innovate courageously, inspire deeply, build wisely, and adapt resiliently. In the grand narrative of human progress, leaders are the authors and architects of tomorrow. Through your vision and action, you turn the unknown into the possible, giving birth to futures that realize the highest aspirations of the human spirit.

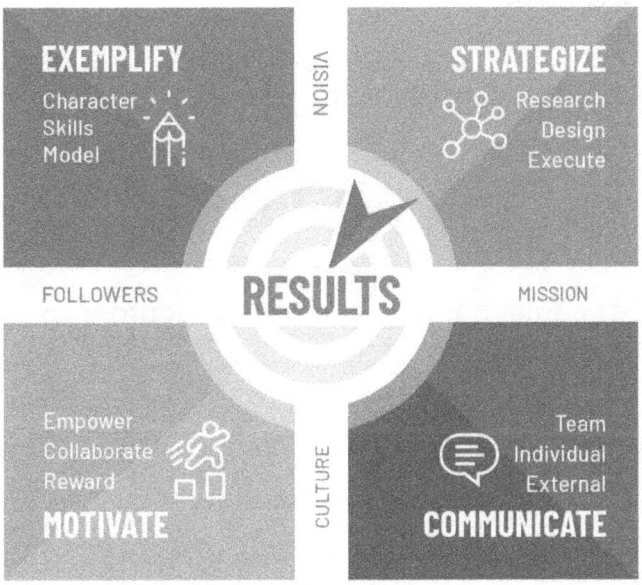

Key Takeaways

- Leadership is fundamentally about creating the future, not just managing the present.
- You create through three primary means: vision, mission, and culture
- Vision requires imagination grounded in reality
- Mission connects daily work to meaningful purpose
- Culture is built through intentional daily choices
- Courage, innovation, and legacy thinking are essential to effective creation

Your Next Steps
- Complete the Vision Development Exercise from this chapter
- Conduct the Culture Audit for your team
- Choose one innovation experiment to launch this month
- Schedule monthly reviews of your progress as a "creator leader"

Questions for Your Team
- What vision do we want to create together?
- How can we make our mission more meaningful and specific?
- What culture do we want to build, and what needs to change to get there?

Now let's explore exactly how to do it, starting with how you exemplify the character, skills, and behaviors that make people want to follow you.

Chapter 2

Exemplify Skills - Mastering the Essential Competencies

You know that sensation when you enter a meeting and can instantly tell if the leader commands the respect of the room? It's not charisma or power—it's something more fundamental. People can sniff authenticity across a conference table, and they can identify a phony just as fast.

As a future-making leader, your character isn't some nice-to-have quality—it's the ground on which all else rests. Your vision is empty promises without character, your mission is manipulation, and your culture is a pretense. But with strong character, you're the kind of leader others wish to be led by, not because they have to, but because they choose to.

Character is the cornerstone of effective leadership. It's what distinguishes a manager from a person others wish to follow. When you exemplify good character, you're not just telling people what to do—you're showing them who to be.

What Character Actually Entails in Leadership

Character isn't perfection. Its authenticity, consistency, and dependability. It's the relationship between what you say you believe and how you actually behave when no one is watching—or when everyone is watching.

Consider the leaders you admire most. What set them apart? It was not their strategic genius or technical expertise alone. It was their character—their integrity, how they treated other people, their consistency in the face of adversity.

Leadership character encompasses several essential factors, but the most central one is integrity. Integrity is being honest and having strong morals. It's the cornerstone that enables everything else.

> **Reflection Questions**
>
> Think about a leader you greatly admire. What are the particular behaviors or decisions that reflected their character? How did these actions affect your willingness to follow them?

Integrity: The Cornerstone of Trust

Integrity at work is the cornerstone on which respect for and trust in your colleagues are established. It is demonstrated by follow-through, being open, and making moral decisions. By doing what you say, whether big or small, you demonstrate reliability and build credibility.

Here is an example of the head of a marketing team at a startup tech company. During a team meeting, he committed to securing approval for new design software by Friday. Thursday afternoon, he found out the approval would be an extra week.

Instead of crossing his fingers, hoping nobody would notice, the man scheduled a quick team meeting right away. "I committed to you to have the software approval by tomorrow, and I won't be able to fulfill it. Here's what happened, here's the new timeline, and here's what I will do to prevent this in the future." That five-minute conversation cost him some short-term embarrassment but earned him long-term credibility. His team learned they could count on not just his commitments, but his integrity when things went wrong.

Here is how integrity manifests itself in real leadership challenges:

- Honor your promises. If you promise to deliver resources for a project, fulfill that promise. If you say you'll have an answer by Tuesday, ensure it's ready by Tuesday—or let them know in advance if there are any changes.

- Be open in your communication. If you communicate openly about challenges and progress, it fosters a culture in which team members feel comfortable expressing their thoughts. Open and honest communication works exceptionally well in challenging conversations, where broaching the issue at hand rather than sidestepping it demonstrates integrity.

- Accept responsibility for errors. If errors occur, take ownership of your failings and learn from them. Rather than blaming others, demonstrate personal accountability by taking responsibility. This fosters a culture of honesty and transparency within the team.

- Ensure confidentiality. Respect confidentiality and safeguard sensitive information. When employees know that their problems and personal details will be kept confidential, it builds a solid foundation of trust, and it is possible to have a more united and integrated working environment.

Practical Activity: Integrity Inventory

Step 1: Commitment Review (15 minutes)
- List down all the promises you've made to your team over the last month
- Tick off what you've kept, what you've broken, and what remains outstanding
- Identify patterns: Do you over-promise? Under-deliver? Communicate changes early?

Step 2: Check for transparency (10 minutes)
- Consider an existing problem your team is dealing with
- Rate your openness about this challenge: 1 (keeping it entirely to yourself) to 10 (being totally open about every aspect)
- What would be the result if you were more open? What are you scared of?

Step 3: Accountability Check (10 minutes)
- Recall your latest significant error or failure.
- How did you handle it? Did you own it immediately or deflect responsibility?
- What did your answer teach your team about accountability?

Step 4: Action Planning (15 minutes)
- Select one area in which you can build your integrity this week
- Name one commitment you must keep or one conversation you must have.
- Create a specific timeline for action.

Demonstrating Competence: Skills That Build Confidence

Character without competence is admirable but ineffective. Your team needs to believe you're a good person and that you are capable of leading them to success. Leadership competence isn't about being the most intelligent person in the room—it's about having the skills and knowledge necessary to guide your team effectively. It is crucial to demonstrate competence as a leader to make informed decisions and provide helpful advice, even in areas you aren't an expert in. Possessing such levels of knowledge will enable you to anticipate problems, spot opportunities, and earn the respect of your team.

Here's an example. A woman was asked to oversee a software development team despite her background in marketing. Rather than pretending to know coding, she spent three months studying the fundamentals: attending daily stand-ups, asking intelligent questions, and taking an online programming course. She didn't become a developer, but she gained sufficient knowledge to comprehend the problems her team encountered, make informed choices about priorities, and communicate authoritatively about technical trade-offs. Her team appreciated her willingness to learn about their world, and her decisions were better because they were grounded in actual knowledge, not assumptions.

Decision-Making Skills

Strong leaders make informed decisions by gathering relevant information, considering multiple perspectives, and evaluating potential outcomes. They're decisive when the time comes to make a decision, and they communicate their rationale with clarity.

Here's how to strengthen your decision-making:
- Gather diverse input. Obtain input from different team members, departments, and stakeholders before making significant decisions.

- Be transparent about your process. When you make a decision, explain the factors you considered and why you chose this path. This helps your team understand your thinking and learn from your approach.

- Own the results. Regardless of whether decisions go well or badly, own the outcome and what you will do differently in the future.

- Learn from failure. If decisions fail, examine what went wrong and pass the lessons on to your crew.

People and Communication Skills

Technical skills are essential, but leadership skills are all about people. You must be proficient in communication, conflict resolution, motivation, and building teams.

Interactive Exercise: Competence Gap Analysis

Part A: Skills Assessment (20 minutes)
Rate yourself (1-10) on these critical leadership competencies:
- Industry/functional knowledge applicable to your team: ___/10
- Strategic thinking and planning: ___/10
- Decision-making under pressure: ___/10
- Communication (speaking, listening, writing): ___/10
- Conflict resolution: ___/10
- Team development and motivation: ___/10
- Change management: ___/10
- Financial awareness applicable to your job: ___/10

Part B: Team Perspective (15 minutes)
Choose three areas where you scored seven or below.
- For every area, ask yourself: In what way does this gap impact your team's faith in your leadership?
- Which deficit, if filled, would make the most significant positive difference in your effectiveness?

Part C: Development Planning (20 minutes)
- Select one skill to focus on improving over the next 90 days
- Specify concrete steps: training, mentoring, practice occasions, and sources of feedback

- Develop a learning plan with weekly targets
- Schedule time for skills development in your diary

Modeling Behavior: Leading by Example

Your team is watching everything you do. They observe how you handle stress, how you communicate with challenging people, how you respond to setbacks, and how you celebrate successes. Whether you realize it or not, you are constantly modeling what leadership is all about.

Behavior modeling demonstrates the behavior you want from your followers. If you want your team to work hard, you must set an example by being a hard worker. To achieve effective communication, you must communicate clearly. If you want accountability, you must be accountable.

The Power of Consistent Modeling

Here's an example: You've said to your team that work-life balance matters and they shouldn't read emails outside of work hours. But you consistently send emails at 10 PM and reply to messages on weekends. What are you actually communicating?

Your actions will always speak louder than your words. Incongruence between word and action doesn't just ruin your credibility—it creates confusion and tension within your team.

For example, consider a man who leads a sales team that has been struggling with the launch of new products. Instead of just telling his team to "learn from failures," he started modeling his own weekly learning reports in team meetings. Each Friday, he'd take a few minutes to talk about something that had gone well that week, one mistake he'd made, what he'd learned from it, and what he'd try differently the following week. Within a month, his team members started reporting their own learning experiences. The culture shifted from hiding mistakes to celebrating learning, and performance improved as people became more willing to experiment and improve.

Key Behaviors to Model

- Work ethic and professionalism. Be punctual, prepared, and focused. Deliver promptly and maintain high standards of personal work.
- Continuous learning. Demonstrate consistent growth by asking questions, seeking feedback, and sharing your learning.
- Respect for others. Treat everyone with dignity, regardless of their position or whether you agree with them.

- Emotional control. Show your team how to handle stress, frustration, and adversity with grace and resilience.

- Accountability. Take responsibility for your mistakes and decisions, and give credit to others for their successes.

Diligence and Communication

These two behaviors deserve special attention because they're fundamental to everything else you do as a leader: diligence and clear communication.

Diligence is being thorough, careful, and persistent in your work. It's about being consistent in showing up, following through, and paying attention to the details that matter. When you exhibit diligence, you're teaching your team that excellence isn't about perfection—it's about caring enough to do it right.

Clear communication means being direct, honest, and thoughtful in how you share information and instructions. It's listening actively, asking clarifying questions, and ensuring understanding before moving forward.

Practical Activity: Behavior Modeling Assessment

Step 1: Determine Your Modeling Gaps (20 minutes)
- List five attitudes or behaviors you require from your team
- For each one, be honest and evaluate: Do you consistently model this behavior?
- Rate yourself 1-10 for each behavior.
- Ask yourself: What would my team members say if they were evaluating me on these very behaviors?

Step 2: Choose Your Focus (10 minutes)
- Choose the behavior for which the discrepancy between expectation and modeling is most significant.
- Or choose the behavior that, if improved, would have the most significant positive impact.

Step 3: Create a Modeling Plan (20 minutes)
- Clearly describe what this behavior would look like in practice
- Identify concrete situations in which you can exhibit this behavior
- Plan how you'll make your modeling visible to your team
- Develop a system to check your consistency (diary, reminders, feedback)

Step 4: Receive Feedback (10 minutes)

> - Select a reliable peer or team member
> - Ask them to help you notice when you are modeling well and when you are not.
> - Arrange a monthly check-in to discuss your progress and advancement.

Character Under Pressure

Anyone can exhibit good character when everything is going their way. It is under pressure—when deadlines are near, when there is conflict, when there is a lot at stake, and when no one would fault you for doing less—that character is truly tested.

These moments of pressure are actually opportunities. They're when your character becomes most visible to your team and when your leadership makes the most significant difference.

Being Consistent When It Is Difficult

Think about this scenario. A woman's team was up against a critical deadline with a major client when they realized they had made a grave mistake in their work that would push delivery back at least a week. So, the woman had a choice: attempt to conceal the delay and hope they could somehow catch up, or call the client immediately and describe what had occurred.

The former might save face in the short term, but could lead to a far larger issue in the long run. The latter was humiliating but truthful. Our example opted for openness. She phoned the client herself, described what had occurred, took complete responsibility, and offered a recovery plan.

The client was initially upset but eventually appreciated the candor and proactive communication. Her team witnessed her model accountability under stress, and it reinforced their confidence in her leadership.

When pressure mounts, remember these principles:
1. Your character is most visible when it costs you something. Easy choices don't demonstrate character. Hard choices do.
2. How you handle stress sets the tone for your team. If you panic, they'll panic. If you stay calm and focused, they'll follow your lead.
3. Pressure exposes priorities. What you are willing to give up when things get tough indicates what you really care about.
4. Recovery is usually more important than perfection. The way you recover from mistakes and setbacks is what teaches your team resilience and responsibility.

> **Reflection Questions**
>
> - When have you been put under stress? How did you react?
> - What does your stress behavior teach your team about leadership?
> - Which character strengths do you wish to cultivate prior to the next crisis occurring?

Building Character Continuously

Character isn't something you have or you don't—it's something you develop and get stronger over time. Like physical fitness, it takes regular effort and practice.

Self-Awareness and Reflection

The foundation of character development is honest self-examination. You need to regularly examine your motives, decisions, and impact on others.

Weekly character reflection questions:
- What were the decisions I made this week that I can be proud of? Why were they correct?

- When did I behave in a manner that was inconsistent with my expressed values? What motivated that decision?
- How did my behavior this week affect my team's trust and respect?
- What character challenge am I currently facing, and how can I grow through it?

Seeking Feedback

Blind spots are dangerous because you're unaware of them. Actively seek feedback from people you trust—peers, mentors, even team members, if your culture allows it.

Ask precise questions:

- "What behaviors do I exhibit that build trust? What behaviors undermine it?"
- "When have you seen me at my best as a leader? What was I doing differently?"
- "If you could change one thing about how I lead, what would it be?"

Continuous Learning

Read about leadership and ethics. Research leaders you respect and leaders who failed. Learn from both positive and negative examples.
- But don't merely read. *Do!*

- Seek out opportunities to flex your character muscles.
- Volunteer for tough conversations.
- Accept challenges that will make you grow.
- Place yourself in situations where your character will be challenged and made strong.

Practical Activity: Personal Character Development Plan

Step 1: Character Evaluation (20 minutes)
- Look over the primary character qualities covered in this chapter: integrity, competence, and modeling.
- Honestly score yourself in each area (1-10)
- List your greatest character strength and your most significant growth opportunity.

Step 2: Feedback Collection (Plan for next 2 weeks)
- Choose three people who can give you honest feedback about your character
- Arrange meetings with all of them
- Prepare challenging questions regarding integrity, competency, and consistency.

Step 3: Development Goals (15 minutes)

- Select one character area to work on for the next 90 days
- Define what success looks like in behavioral terms
- List scenarios in which you can practice and develop this skill

Step 4: Accountability System (10 minutes)
- Establish a weekly reflection practice (e.g., calendar reminder, diary).
- Choose someone to be an accountability partner
- Schedule monthly reviews of your character development progress

The Character-Trust Link

Everything we've discussed in this chapter points to one significant outcome: trust. Character builds trust, and trust is what makes leadership possible.

If your team trusts you, they'll stick with you through ambiguity, provide the benefit of the doubt when things don't go as expected, and put forth their best effort toward a common goal. If you don't have trust, you aren't really leading—you're merely managing compliance.

Your team establishes trust through hundreds of minor interactions over time. Each conversation, each decision, and each stress response either builds or erodes trust. There are no neutral moments in leadership.

The trust equation for leaders:

Credibility (competence + reliability)

+

Intimacy (safety + care)

-

Self-Orientation (ego + self-interest)

=

Trust

Your character has a direct impact on each component of this formula. Integrity establishes credibility. Competence gives others confidence in your competence. Consistency establishes safety. Including others' interests with your own minimizes the perception of selfish intent.

Trust Assessment Exercise

For each person on your team, consider:
- Do they approach you with issues and problems? (Reflects safety/intimacy)
- Do they comply with enthusiasm or just follow your orders? (Indicates credibility)
- Do they speak positively about you to others? (Indicates general trust)
- Do they come to you with their finest thoughts and proposals? (Shows respect and safety)

Red flags that indicate low trust:
- Individuals inform you of just what you wish to listen to
- Team members work around you to get things done
- You hear about problems from others instead of from your team
- People seem uninterested or do only enough to pass

If there is low trust, ask yourself:
- Where has my character been inconsistent?
- What obligations have I broken or failed to fulfill?

- When have I acted in my own interest at the expense of my team?
- What are some particular behaviors that can express trustworthiness?

Wrapping It Up

Character is not only the first chapter of leadership—it's the foundation upon which every other leadership skill is made effective. Your vision is worthless if people don't trust your motives. Your communication is meaningless if people doubt your integrity. Your ability to motivate is based squarely on your credibility. And if you consistently demonstrate integrity, competency, and sincere behavior, you're the kind of leader people will want to follow. You're the kind of person who can inspire others not just to do the job, but to be their best.

Character is also how you demonstrate what's possible. When your team observes you behaving with integrity under pressure, they learn that integrity is possible for them too. When they observe you owning mistakes, they discover that vulnerability is a strength. When they observe you learning and improving continuously, they realize that improvement is always possible.

This is the reason why demonstrating character is so core to the leader as creator. You are not only envisioning a future vision or strategy—you are imagining the types of individuals who can create that future. And it begins with making your best self.

Key Takeaways:

- Character is the foundation that makes all other leadership skills effective.
- Integrity generates trust by being consistent in values and practices
- Competence creates confidence in your ability to lead effectively
- Behavioral modeling teaches your team what positive leadership looks like.
- Character is most clearly tested and revealed under pressure
- Trust is the end result of long-term, consistent character

Your Next Steps:

- Take the Integrity Inventory to identify areas for improvement
- Conduct the Competence Gap Analysis and create a development plan

- Evaluate your behavior modeling and select one area to improve
- Develop a weekly character reflection routine
- Ask colleagues you trust for their opinion of your character and dependability.

Questions for Your Team:

Which leadership behaviors earn your trust most readily?

When have you observed leadership character under stress? What did you learn?

How can we foster greater accountability and integrity within our team culture? Keep in mind: Character is not about perfection—it is about authenticity, consistency, and a commitment to improvement. Each new day provides opportunities to reinforce your character and enhance the trust in your leadership that your team has.

In the following chapter, we will learn how to develop and demonstrate the technical and strategic competencies that enhance your character and facilitate your effectiveness as a more powerful leader.

Chapter 3

Exemplify Skills - Mastering the Essential Competencies

You've gained trust through your character. Your followers believe in your integrity and your consistency. But character alone is not enough to lead effectively. People also need to think that you know what you're doing—that you have the skills and competency to lead them to success.

Leadership is an art that demands a multifaceted set of skills to influence, motivate, and guide people and organizations in attaining their objectives. In the modern, rapidly evolving, and dynamic business world, successful leaders require not only technical competence but also strategic acumen. This chapter examines the essential technical and strategic skills leaders must develop to achieve success and effectiveness in their roles.

Consider skills as the instruments in your leadership toolbox. Character gets individuals to believe in you, while skills make them sure that you can actually deliver results. Without both, you're either a decent individual who can't get things done or an able individual nobody wishes to follow.

> ### Reflection Question
> Consider a leader whom you admire as both a person and a professional. What particular skills did the leader exhibit that assured you they were capable of leading? In what ways did those skills enhance their character?

Technical Skills: Understanding the Work You Oversee

Technical skills refer to the specialized knowledge and expertise required to perform the duties associated with a specific line of work or industry. Leaders need these skills to comprehend the details of their job, make sound judgments, and earn the respect and trust of their employees.

You don't need to be the leading technician among your people, but you need to know enough to make credible decisions, ask thoughtful questions, and recognize when something isn't working. Next are the key technical skills leaders need to learn:

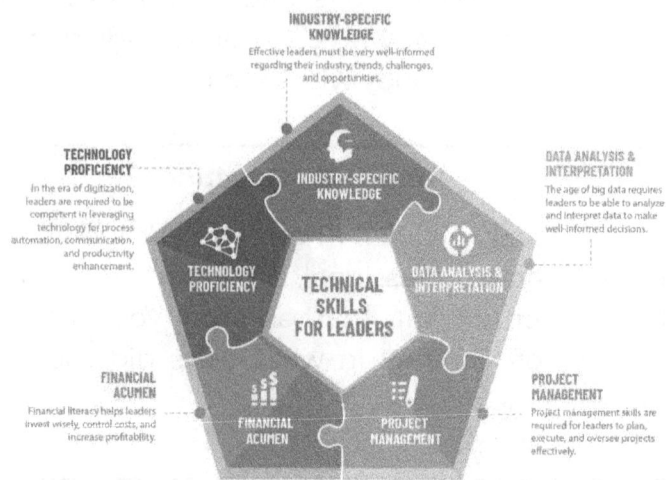

Industry-Specific Knowledge

Effective leaders must be well-informed about their industry, including trends, challenges, and opportunities. By being well-informed, leaders can make informed decisions, anticipate market changes, and stay ahead of their competitors. Leaders must remain current by reading industry journals, attending conferences, and networking with peers.

For example, a tech industry leader should be aware of the latest developments in artificial intelligence and cyber threats, and understand the implications of these technologies for their company. You don't have to write the code for the next breakthrough, but you must know what these advancements spell for your organization and team.

Here's another example. Consider the case of a bank branch manager who must be well-versed in banking laws, financial instruments, and customer relationship management strategies. Knowing the details of loan processing, risk analysis, and adherence to financial regulations enables them to make sound decisions that are favorable to both the bank and the customers. Moreover, being aware of recent developments in digital banking and fintech solutions can enable managers to enhance branch offerings and increase customer satisfaction.

The trick is knowing enough to:

- Ask the right questions when your team presents you with problems
- Know the consequences of decisions before making them

- Identify opportunities and threats that others may overlook
- Speak credibly to stakeholders, customers, and senior leadership

---

Practical Activity: Test of Industry Knowledge

Step 1: Current Knowledge Audit (20 minutes)
- Give the top 5 trends currently affecting your field
- Enumerate three major issues your industry will encounter within the next 2 years
- Identify two emerging opportunities that would be beneficial to your organization
- Rate your knowledge in each area: 1 (minimal) to 10 (expert level)

Step 2: Knowledge Gap Analysis (15 minutes)
- Which areas were below 7? These are your priority learning areas
- What are some decisions you have made lately that would have been improved by having more industry insight?
- Where do your team members have expertise that you could learn from?

Step 3: Learning Plan (20 minutes)
- Select two areas of industry knowledge to target this quarter

> - Specify exact sources: publications, experts, courses, conferences
> - Plan a dedicated learning time in your schedule (minimum 2 hours/week)
> - Plan how you will apply this knowledge in real-life situations

Data Analysis and Interpretation

In the era of big data, analytical and interpretive skills in data are crucial for making informed decisions. Leaders must be proficient in the use of data analytics tools and techniques to extract insights, identify trends, and measure performance effectively. This helps them make data-informed decisions that can lead their organization to success and growth.

For instance, a marketing executive can utilize data analytics to monitor customer behavior, quantify campaign effectiveness, and streamline marketing initiatives to achieve improved outcomes. You do not have to be a data scientist, but you must be comfortable asking the proper questions about data and understanding the implications of the responses.

What does data literacy for leaders look like?
- Knowing what metrics really count for your objectives

- Understanding when information is accurate and when it is deceptive
- Capacity to identify trends and patterns that guide strategy
- Asking data quality and methodological probing questions
- Translating data insights into actionable decisions

Project Management

Practical project management skills are essential for leaders to plan, execute, and oversee projects efficiently. These include establishing project goals, creating timetables, allocating resources, and avoiding risks. Knowledge of project management tools and methodologies, such as Microsoft Project, Agile, and Scrum, can allow leaders to complete projects on time and on budget (Sliger, 2011).

A leader managing a product launch, for example, must coordinate teams, oversee the production timeline, and troubleshoot problems that arise along the way. Even when you have separate project managers, you must grasp the fundamentals of project management to offer helpful guidance and assistance.

Key project management skills for executives:

- Dividing large initiatives into more miniature stages
- Identifying and coordinating dependencies between different work streams
- Balancing conflicting priorities and resources
- Communicating progress and challenges clearly to stakeholders
- Adjusting plans as situations evolve

Financial Acumen

A solid understanding of financial concepts is essential for leaders to make informed business decisions. These include budgeting, forecasting, economic analysis, and reading financial statements. Financial literacy enables leaders to invest wisely, manage costs effectively, and enhance profitability.

For example, a manufacturing company leader needs to understand cost structures, pricing, and financial metrics to maintain the company's financial health. You do not need to be a CFO, but you need to be able to speak the language of business.

Key financial skills for leaders:

- Reading and comprehending simple financial reports

- Understanding how your decisions impact the bottom line
- Developing and working with budgets efficiently
- Assessing ROI on initiatives and investments
- Identifying financial warning signs prior to their becoming crises

Interactive Exercise: Financial Fluency Check

Assess your preparedness for financial leadership:
- Can you describe your department's budget in layman's terms? Yes/No
- Do you know the top 3 cost drivers in your area? Yes/No
- Can you calculate the ROI of a typical project you oversee? Yes/No
- Do you understand how your team's work affects company profitability? Yes/No
- Can you identify early warning signs of budget problems? Yes/No

Scoring:
- 5 Yes: Strong financial leadership foundation
- 3-4 Yes: Good fundamentals, potential to develop
- 1-2 Yes: Priority development area
- 0 Yes: Start with financial fundamentals immediately

Development activities based on your score:
- If 3+ Yes: Focus on strategic financial planning and complex financial analysis
- If 1-2 Yes: Complete a business finance course and collaborate with your finance team
- If 0 Yes: Have monthly meetings with finance to learn the basics

Strategic Skills: Thinking Ahead of Today

Strategic skills encompass the capacity for critical thinking, future planning, and decision-making that align with the organization's long-term objectives. These are the skills leaders need to navigate complex settings, capitalize on opportunities, and spearhead environmental sustainability and growth. The following are the major strategic skills leaders need to cultivate:

Visionary Thinking

Successful leaders have the capacity to envision a desirable and attractive future for their organization. This includes establishing long-term objectives, recognizing expansion opportunities, and developing a plan to realize the vision. Visionary leadership enables leaders to inspire their staff members and direct their efforts towards a shared goal.

For instance, a CEO who wants their business to be a market leader in renewable energy may emphasize innovation, strategic alliances, and sustainability to realize their vision. But visionary thinking is not only for CEO's—every leader must look beyond existing limitations to envision what is feasible.

Developing your visionary thinking:
- Occasionally, step back from day-to-day operations to consider broader picture trends
- Study how other industries solve similar problems
- Ask "What would be possible if...?" questions
- Link current competencies to future possibilities
- Challenge assumptions about what's "realistic"

Strategic Planning

Strategic planning is the act of determining an organization's direction and making resource allocation decisions to follow that direction. Leaders need to be skilled at developing strategic plans that detail the organization's goals, objectives, and action plans. This involves conducting a SWOT analysis (Strengths, Weaknesses, Opportunities, and Threats), prioritizing tasks, and tracking progress.

A leader in a healthcare organization, for example, might craft a strategic plan to develop new services, enhance patient care, and improve operational efficiency. Strategic planning is not simply the generation of documents, but rather the methodical consideration of how to achieve important goals.

Strategic planning components every leader should master:
- Situation analysis: Understanding current reality clearly
- Goal setting: Defining specific, measurable outcomes
- Resource allocation: Deciding where to allocate time, money, and energy
- Risk assessment: Determining what might go wrong and how to prevent it
- Progress monitoring: Tracking whether your plan is working

Practical Activity: Strategic Thinking Development

Step 1: Strategic Questions Practice (25 minutes)
For your present team/department, respond to these questions:
- What would success look like for us in three years?
- What external trends could most impact our work?
- What are our particular strengths that we might utilize more?
- What threats could derail our progress?
- What would we do differently if resources were not a limitation?

Step 2: Strategic Option Generation (20 minutes)
- From your responses above, list three strategic options for your team
- For every choice, indicate the needed resources, possible advantages, and principal risks
- Consider which choice optimizes opportunity and feasibility?

Step 3: Strategic Communication (15 minutes)
- Practice explaining your selected strategic direction in 2 minutes or less

> - Provide: where you're headed, why it's important, what it will require
> - Give it a go: Would this vision inspire and be understandable to your team?

Decision-Making

Effective decision-making is the ability to assess alternatives, consider potential consequences, and select courses of action that are in the best interest of the organization.

Leaders need strong critical thinking skills to assess complex situations, weigh the advantages and disadvantages, and make informed decisions. This competency is crucial for managing uncertainty and making informed decisions that drive organizational success.

For example, a crisis leader must rapidly analyze the situation, weigh the effects of different actions, and make timely decisions to reduce risks. Effective decision-making blends analytical thinking with practical wisdom.

Components of successful leadership decision-making:
- Collecting pertinent information without paralysis of analysis

- Considering multiple perspectives and potential consequences
- Making decisions with partial information when necessary
- Communicating decisions clearly and explaining the reasoning
- Learning from both good and bad decisions

Change Management

In a changing business world, leaders must be competent change managers. This involves comprehending the effects of change, communication, and leading their team members through changes. Change management competencies enable leaders to adopt new strategies, processes, and technologies with less resistance and maintain morale intact.

For instance, a leader who introduces a new software system in their organization must communicate the advantages, offer training, and assist workers throughout the transition. Change is a regular part of life nowadays, and thus change management is a vital leadership skill.

Change management principles:
- Understanding why change is necessary and explaining that "why"

- Anticipating resistance and addressing concerns proactively
- Dividing significant changes into smaller steps
- Offering support and training during the transition
- Celebrating success and learning from failure

Problem-Solving

Leaders must be adept at recognizing problems, conducting root cause analysis, and formulating solutions. This requires a combination of analytical skill, creativity, and thinking outside the box. Practical problem-solving skills enable leaders to be proactive in addressing challenges and to preempt problems before they become unmanageable.

For example, a logistics industry leader may need to resolve supply chain breakdowns by identifying secondary suppliers, streamlining routes, and implementing contingency measures. Problem-solving is an everyday leadership task—the more you practice it, the more efficient you will be.

Problem-solving approach for leaders:
- Specifically define the problem (what exactly is wrong?)
- Gather relevant information (what do we know and not know?)

- Generate several possible solutions (what are our options?)
- Evaluate solutions against criteria (what will work best?)
- Execute the selected solution (how do we make it happen?)
- Monitor results and adjust where required (is it working?)

Interpersonal Skills: The Human Side of Leadership

In addition to strategic and technical capabilities, effective leaders must possess solid interpersonal skills to build relationships, influence others, and foster a positive work environment. These are the skills that typically set good leaders apart from great ones.

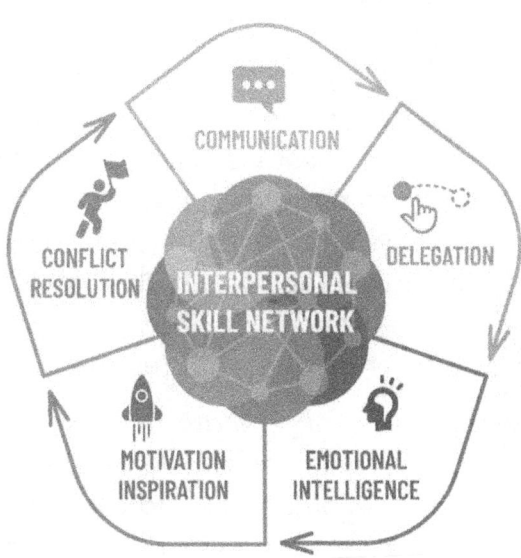

Communication

Effective and clear communication is essential for leaders to convey their vision, objectives, and expectations to their team members. This encompasses verbal and written communication, as well as listening. Practical communication skills enable leaders to establish trust, resolve disagreements, and ensure that they and their team members are all aligned.

For instance, a leader who holds team meetings should clearly state the agenda, invite open discussion, and listen attentively to feedback from team members.

The elements of leadership communication include:
- *Active listening* is one key aspect of effective communication. It involves providing one's undivided attention, understanding, responding, and remembering what is communicated. Leaders who listen actively demonstrate to their team members that they are genuinely interested in their input and concerned about their views. This can lead to a more engaged and motivated team because members feel heard and appreciated.
- *Nonverbal communication* is equally important. Leaders must be mindful of their posture, facial expressions, and eye contact, as these can convey confidence, openness, and

attentiveness. Positive nonverbal cues can reinforce verbal messages and foster a sense of rapport with team members. For instance, maintaining eye contact and nodding while conversing can indicate that the leader is listening and genuinely interested in what is being said.

- *Feedback* is also a key component of effective communication. Providing constructive feedback informs members of their strengths and areas for improvement, and it encourages personal and professional growth. Effective leaders provide feedback in a considerate and constructive manner, citing specific behaviors and offering targeted developmental recommendations. Conducting regular feedback sessions can help identify issues early and resolve them before they escalate.

Additionally, leaders must be skilled at communicating effectively in various contexts, including one-on-one meetings, team meetings, and public speaking. Each context requires a distinct style and set of skills. For instance, in one-on-one sessions, a leader may attempt to establish a personal rapport and discuss personal issues. In contrast, in team meetings, they may emphasize teamwork and collaborative problem-solving. In conclusion, communication is a complex skill that includes verbal, nonverbal, and written aspects. Through the mastery of these skills, leaders can articulate their vision, establish good relationships, and foster a good and productive working environment.

Emotional Intelligence

Emotional intelligence (EI) refers to the ability to perceive, understand, and manage one's own emotions as well as the emotions of others. Leaders with high EI are empathetic, self-aware, and have strong relationship skills. Emotional intelligence enables leaders to relate to their followers, understand their needs, and offer a conducive working environment.

Certain key aspects of emotional intelligence pertain particularly to leaders:

- *Self-awareness:* This is the ability to acknowledge and be conscious of one's own emotions and thoughts. Self-aware leaders are better equipped to manage stress and make informed decisions. For instance, a self-aware leader may notice feelings of being overwhelmed and step back to reorganize priorities.

- *Self-regulation refers to the capacity to manage or redirect disruptive impulses and emotions and adjust to changing* situations. Leaders who self-regulate do not allow emotions to dictate their behavior and remain unflustered in the face of pressure. For example, a leader who stays calm during an argumentative meeting is more likely to diffuse conflict successfully.

- *Motivation:* Leaders with high EI are driven to exceed expectations. They are passionate about their job, set high standards for themselves and others, and are determined to overcome hurdles. A motivational leader might inspire their staff by setting a clear vision and marking progress along the way.

- *Empathy:* Empathy is the ability to be sensitive to the feelings of others and consider their emotions while making any decision. An empathetic leader can step into the shoes of his/her team members, making the work environment more open and supportive. For example, a leader who patiently listens to an employee's concerns and helps to solve them is empathetic.

- *Social skills*: These are the tools used to manage relationships in a way that achieves a positive outcome. Socially skilled leaders are effective communicators, skilled conflict resolvers, and adept at building networks. A leader with excellent social skills is equipped to build a strong team.

For instance, a leader who demonstrates empathy during moments of hardship can enhance team spirit and give a feeling of belonging. A leader who recognizes the difficulties their team is facing and provides the necessary support can strengthen the team's resilience and commitment. Emotional intelligence is not a luxury trait; it is a necessity for effective leadership and can be a major contributor to an organization's success.

Interactive Exercise: Emotional Intelligence Self-Assessment

Rate yourself (1-10) on each EI component:

Self-Awareness:
- I recognize my emotional triggers: ___/10
- I know how my feelings influence my choices: ___/10
- I'm aware of my impact on others: ___/10
- Self-Regulation:
- I remain calm when under pressure: ___/10
- I think before I act emotionally: ___/10
- I adapt well to changing circumstances: ___/10

Motivation:
- I keep going despite setbacks: ___/10
- I have high expectations of myself: ___/10
- I'm driven by more than external rewards: ___/10

Empathy:
- I correctly interpret other people's feelings: ___/10

> - I consider others' feelings in my decisions: ___/10
> - I understand different perspectives: ___/10
>
> Social Skills:
> - I easily build rapport: ___/10
> - I handle conflicts constructively: ___/10
> - I influence others positively: ___/10
>
> Development Focus:
> - Identify your lowest-scoring section
> - Choose one of these behaviors to practice this week
> - Request a colleague you trust to provide you with feedback in this regard

Delegation

Delegation is the ability to assign tasks and responsibility to team members in accordance with their strengths and levels of competence. Effective delegation enables leaders to focus on strategic priorities while providing team members with the opportunity to take ownership of their work.

It is an essential skill for maximizing productivity and developing the skills and abilities of team members.

Leaders need to be aware of each team member's strengths, weaknesses, and potential so they can delegate properly. This enables them to match the best-suited tasks to the best-suited people so all team members can work to their utmost capabilities. Leaders also need to provide clear instructions and expectations, along with the necessary tools and assistance. This keeps team members informed and provides them with the essential information to complete their assigned tasks successfully.

Furthermore, effective delegation also involves following up on progress and providing ongoing feedback to ensure continued success. Leaders must follow up with their team members to track their progress, address any challenges that arise, and provide guidance as needed. This not only keeps the project on track but also allows for learning and growth.

Delegation is not just about assigning tasks; it also involves building trust and confidence within the team. Leaders should encourage open communication and create an environment where team members feel comfortable asking questions and sharing their ideas. Recognizing and rewarding the efforts and achievements of team members can also boost morale and motivation.

For instance, a project manager assigning tasks to team members according to their expertise can help the project move forward smoothly and effectively. By providing clear guidelines, required resources, and ongoing support, the project manager can empower team members to take responsibility for their own tasks. Periodic check-ins and feedback can help resolve any problems immediately and keep the project on track. Team victories can be celebrated, and individual efforts can be recognized to promote motivation and teamwork further.

Ultimately, delegation is a critical leadership skill that involves more than simply assigning tasks. It requires knowledge of team members' capabilities, providing explicit instruction and resources, monitoring, feedback, and fostering trust within the team. Leaders can effectively enhance productivity, team development, and the achievement of organizational goals by mastering the art of delegation.

Conflict Resolution

Leaders must be adept at resolving conflicts and managing disagreements among their group members. This requires them to understand different perspectives, foster open communication, and arrive at mutually acceptable solutions. Conflict resolution skills are crucial for leaders to maintain harmony and cooperation within their teams.

For example, a leader mediating a dispute among team members should promote open communication, seek common ground, and strive for a solution that benefits everyone involved. This can be achieved through active listening, recognizing emotions, and fostering a culture of respect and understanding among team members.

Additionally, conflict resolution is not only about resolving conflicts once they have occurred, but also about preventing conflicts from arising in the first place. This can be done by clearly defining expectations, fostering a culture of openness, and facilitating proactive communication.

Motivation and Inspiration

Effective leaders possess the ability to influence and inspire their team members to deliver their best. This includes rewarding and recognizing accomplishments, offering constructive feedback, and creating a positive working environment. Motivated and inspired team members are more efficient, engaged, and committed to the organization's success.

For instance, a leader who celebrates team victories and offers opportunities for growth can enhance team morale and performance. This can be accomplished by regularly recognizing employees, offering opportunities for personal development, and fostering a sense of belonging and purpose within the team.

Moreover, motivational leaders lead by example, modeling the values and behaviors they expect from their people. They take a genuine interest in the welfare and growth of their people, creating a climate in which all feel valued and encouraged to contribute.

Practical Activity: Skills Development Action Plan

Step 1: Skills Assessment (30 minutes)
Reflect on all the skills addressed in this chapter and score yourself:
Technical Skills: (1-10 each)
- Industry knowledge: ___
- Data analysis: ___
- Project management: ___
- Financial acumen: ___
- Technology proficiency: ___

Strategic Skills: (1-10 each)
- Visionary thinking: ___
- Strategic planning: ___
- Decision-making: ___
- Change management: ___

- Problem-solving: ___

Interpersonal Skills: (1-10 each)
- Communication: ___
- Emotional intelligence: ___
- Delegation: ___
- Conflict resolution: ___
- Motivation/inspiration: ___

Step 2: Setting Priorities (15 minutes)
- List your top 3 strengths (highest scores)
- List your top 3 development needs (lowest scores or most significant gaps)
- Reflect: Which skill, if enhanced, would make the most significant difference in your effectiveness?

Step 3: Development Planning (20 minutes)
Choose ONE skill to focus on for the next 90 days:
- Specific learning objectives
- Learning materials (courses, books, mentors)
- Practice opportunities
- Success measures
- Timeline and milestones

The Integration Challenge

The real leadership challenge is *integrating* these skills after mastering them. Technical skills give you credibility, strategic skills enable you to see the big picture, and interpersonal skills allow you to work through people. Yet outstanding leaders seem to integrate all three with ease.

Here is an example. A woman leads a customer service team during a period of rapid expansion. When call volume increased 40% and customer satisfaction levels dropped, she summoned all her experience:

- Technical skills: She analyzed call data to identify peak times and common issues
- Strategic skills: She came up with a strategy to recruit and train new employees and enhance processes
- Interpersonal skills: She encouraged her current staff through the stressful time while providing confidence to recruits

The integration of these skills—not any single skill alone—enabled her to manage the challenge successfully.

Developing Skill Integration

- Practice situational leadership. Different situations require different skill combinations. Learn to diagnose what each situation needs and adapt your approach accordingly.

- Get feedback on your integration. Ask colleagues not only about individual competencies, but about how you integrate them into actual situations.
- Observe other leaders. Take note of how effective leaders in your organization combine different skills. What do you notice as patterns?
- Look back at your experiences. Following difficult experiences, examine which skills you employed well and which you might have used more effectively.

Skills as a Foundation for Future Growth

Effective leaders are lifelong learners who constantly seek to improve themselves and adapt to new challenges. They understand that leadership is not a position but a process that requires continuous development and growth. Leaders can have a lasting impact on their organizations and the world by investing in their own skills and competencies.

This in-depth examination of the technical and strategic skills required for successful leadership highlights the complexity of leadership. Whereas technical skills provide the foundation for understanding the complexities of work, strategic skills enable leaders to envision and prepare for the future. Interpersonal skills, however, are the cement that binds it all together, facilitating teamwork, trust, and motivation among the staff.

As the business world continues to evolve, the demand for these skills will only grow stronger. Leaders who can harmonize technical ability, strategic direction, and interpersonal skills will be well-positioned to conquer the challenges of the modern world and lead their organizations to new heights of success.

Key Takeaways

- Technical skill constitutes the foundation of successful leadership
- Strategic skills enable long-term thinking and planning
- Interpersonal skills make everything else possible through people
- It is the combination of all three types of skills that distinguishes great leaders from good leaders. Ongoing learning and skills acquisition are crucial to leadership effectiveness.

Your Next Steps

- Complete the comprehensive skills evaluation
- Choose one skill area to develop for the next 90 days

- Develop a specific development plan with resources and milestones
- Ask colleagues for feedback on your present skill efficacy
- Seek opportunities to practice integrating skills into real-life situations

Questions for Your Team

- What skills do you most value in leaders you've worked with?
- Where do you think there are opportunities for me to improve my leadership abilities?
- How can I better support your growth and skill development?

Keep in mind that skills without character are hollow, but character without skills cannot deliver. Together, they are the foundation of leaders whom people not only trust but willingly follow to a shared goal.

In the coming chapter, we will discuss how to model the behaviors. We will examine several real-world examples and discuss how to integrate these tips into our own practices effectively.

Chapter 4

Leading by Example - Modeling at Every Level

You have effectively characterized yourself and demonstrated your competence. Your followers trust you and believe in your potential. But they're still asking themselves one very critical question: "Will you actually walk the talk?"

Behavior modeling is where leadership becomes tangible. It's the distinction between telling individuals what to do and demonstrating how to be. Daily, in a million little moments, you're either supporting or negating all you've spoken regarding values, standards, and expectations.

The reality is your team is observing everything you do. They observe how you handle stress, how you interact with challenging individuals, how you respond to failures, and how you celebrate successes. Whether you know it or not, you're consistently modeling what leadership at all levels of the company looks like.

In this chapter, we'll cover how to model wanted leadership behavior at each level of management. The well-defined hierarchy of the banking industry will be used to show how modeling can be accomplished in any organization. We'll cover what modeling at the executive, middle management, and front-line leadership levels is—and how you can model the behaviors that will make others want to follow you.

> **Reflection Questions**
>
> Consider a leader whose example you've attempted to follow. What did they specifically do that you wished to copy? In what ways did their example shape your own leadership?

Leadership Levels and Modeling Responsibilities: Understanding

The sophisticated and multifaceted banking industry relies heavily on a structured management hierarchy for its smooth functionality, adherence to regulations, and customer satisfaction. The hierarchical structure in the banking industry comprises various levels, each with distinct responsibilities and roles. It is essential for individuals who aspire to instill solid leadership traits that trickle down through an organization to learn about these levels.

What is especially instructive about leadership modeling in this hierarchy is the way behavior and expectations trickle down from the top to the bottom. Each level not only oversees the level beneath them—they model what leadership should be at every level of an organization.

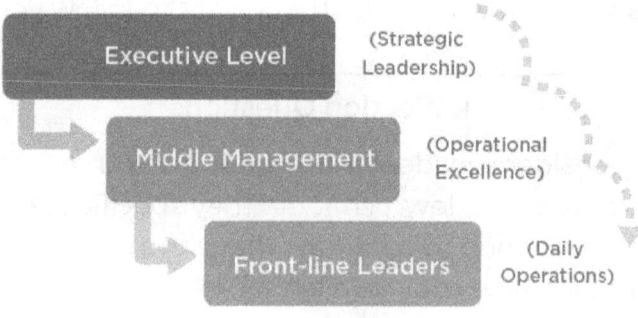

Here is an example to think about. At a regional bank, a CEO went out of his way to visit branches quarterly and spend time with front-line staff. Not only was this good PR, but it also modeled the behavior he wanted to see from every leader. Before long, VPs were visiting branches monthly, regional managers were visiting branches more often, and branch managers were spending more time on the floor with their staff. The CEO's modeling behavior triggered a cascade of more visible and engaged leadership across the organization.

Top-Level Management: Modeling Strategic Leadership

At the top of the bank's hierarchy are the upper-level management, which chiefly comprises the Board of Directors, the Chief Executive Officer (CEO), and other C-level executives, such as the Chief Financial Officer (CFO), Chief Operating Officer (COO), and Chief Risk Officer (CRO).

Executive Leadership Modeling

The Board of Directors models governance and oversight by establishing the organization's strategic direction, making the main policy decisions, and overseeing executive management. The shareholders elect them and are accountable for ensuring that the organization operates in the best interest of its clients as well as stakeholders.

The Chief Executive Officer (CEO) sets an example for the organization by implementing the board's strategies and policies. They oversee overall operations, make important decisions, and serve as the primary spokesperson. The CEO establishes the organizational culture and vision through their daily actions and decisions.

Other C-suite Executives model functional excellence by supporting the CEO in managing various aspects of operations. For instance, the CFO models financial stewardship through budgeting, forecasting, and financial planning. The COO models operational excellence by ensuring processes run smoothly, while the CRO models risk awareness by identifying, assessing, and mitigating risks.

Leadership Behaviors to Model at the Executive Level

To excel at the top management level, C-suite executives must model a unique set of leadership behaviors that enable them to function effectively in complex organizational settings. These behaviors allow them to make effective decisions, engage their workforce, and drive the organization toward its strategic goals.

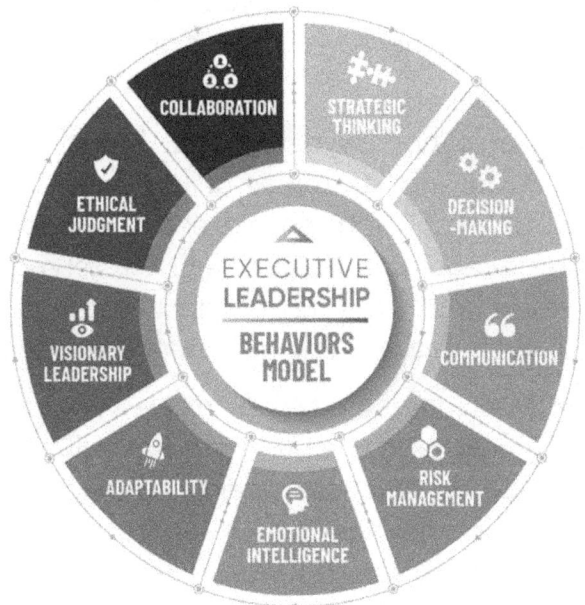

- Strategic Thinking: The C-suite leaders need to role-model long-term thinking by actively scanning market trends, foreseeing changes, and determining opportunities for innovation and growth. This includes posing strategic questions in meetings, communicating market insights to the organization, and demonstrating how everyday choices align with long-term goals.

- Decision-Making: Demonstrate high-level decision-making by assessing intricate situations openly, taking into account different viewpoints candidly, and making choices that evidently support organizational values and objectives. Demonstrate your decision-making process, not merely your decisions.

- Communication: Model exemplary communication by being clear in articulating the vision and strategies of the organization, both internally with employees and externally with stakeholders. Practice active listening and develop the skills to connect with diverse audiences in a genuine and meaningful way.

- Risk Management: Model risk awareness by openly discussing potential risks, illustrating how you assess their impact, and demonstrating how you mitigate them. This maintains organizational stability and resilience.

- Emotional Intelligence: Demonstrate emotional intelligence by being self-aware, self-regulating, empathetic, and having social skills. Demonstrate how to develop strong relationships, constructively resolve conflicts, and establish a positive organizational culture through your day-to-day interactions.

- Adaptability: Demonstrate adaptability by openly accepting change and guiding teams through it with ease. Be comfortable with ambiguity and model how to adjust when situations shift.

- Visionary Leadership: Demonstrate visionary thinking by establishing a clear direction, building a sense of purpose, and promoting innovation through your own curiosity and receptivity to new ideas.

- Ethical Judgment: Demonstrate steadfast ethical principles by integrity, transparency, and accountability in every action. Ensure the organization conducts its business in accordance with applicable laws and regulations while maintaining its reputation.

- Collaboration: Model collaboration by collaborating with transparency with peers and stakeholders, building teamwork, promoting cross-functional collaboration, and using diverse perspectives visibly.

Practical Activity: Executive Modeling Evaluation

Step 1: Visibility Audit (20 minutes)
Think about your present position and respond:
- How visible are your strategic thinking processes to your organization?
- When did you last model decision-making transparency?
- How do others see you handling stress, conflict, and change?
- What are you doing that others might be copying?

Step 2: Gap Analysis Modeling (15 minutes)
- List 5 behaviors you expect from your leadership team
- Rate how well you model each behavior (1-10)
- Identify the most significant mismatch between expectation and model

Step 3: Modeling Action Plan (20 minutes)
- Choose two behaviors you would like to model more intentionally
- Identify specific scenarios in which you can exhibit these behaviors
- Specify how you will make your modeling more observable to others
- Set reminders to check your modeling consistency

These leadership actions are crucial for C-suite leaders to navigate organizational complexities, drive success, and maintain stakeholder trust. By consistently demonstrating these traits with transparency, they can successfully guide the organization toward sustainable growth and innovation.

Middle-Level Management: Modeling Operational Excellence

Middle management serves as a bridge between the top leadership and the lower-level employees. It is made up of Vice Presidents (VPs), Assistant Vice Presidents (AVPs), and Regional Managers who must lead by example in translating strategy into action.

Operational Oversight Modeling

Vice Presidents (VPs) set an example for departmental leadership by leading individual departments or regions of the organization. They set an example of how to execute strategies designed by upper management while making their departments achieve performance expectations. They illustrate decision-making and indicate participation in high-level planning and coordination.

Assistant Vice Presidents (AVPs) set the example for tactical implementation by assisting VPs in overseeing their departments. They set the example for day-to-day operational management, regulatory adherence, and enhancing operational effectiveness. AVPs practice hands-on management and demonstrate how to implement strategies tactically.

Regional Managers set an example of local leadership by overseeing operations in particular geographic locations. They set an example of how to maintain compliance with organizational policies and procedures, achieve performance targets, and deliver quality customer service. Regional Managers also set an example of local market growth and community involvement.

Leadership Behaviors for Middle-Level Managers to Emulate

Middle managers play a crucial role in translating the strategic intent of top managers into concrete plans and overseeing their successful implementation. To be successful in this key role,

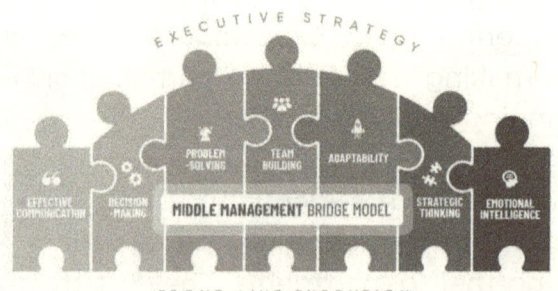

middle managers must exhibit a diverse range of leadership behaviors.

- Effective Communication: Model effective communication by showing how to communicate strategies and goals from upper management to teams. Demonstrate active listening and give constructive feedback to team members, fostering an atmosphere of open communication and respect.

- Decision-Making: Demonstrate analytical decision-making by clearly considering the pros and cons of different alternatives, weighing possible effects on departments and the institution, and making informed decisions that align with organizational goals.

- Problem-Solving: Model problem-solving by illustrating how to identify problems early, generate creative solutions, and implement them successfully to maintain continuous operations.

- Team Building: Exhibit exemplary team building by recognizing and leveraging individual strengths, fostering collaboration, and facilitating positive and inclusive working relationships in your daily interactions.

- Adaptability: Exhibit flexibility by being receptive to new ideas openly, indicating a willingness to absorb new technologies and processes, and leading teams through change with visible confidence and resilience.

- Emotional Intelligence: Role-model emotional awareness by showing understanding and control of your own emotions and empathy towards team members. Establish strong relationships, manage conflict successfully, and develop a caring work culture.

- Strategic Thinking: Model strategic awareness by illustrating how to forecast future trends, recognize improvement opportunities, and connect departmental activities to larger organizational objectives while sustaining operational focus.

> ### Interactive Exercise: Middle Management Modeling Challenge
>
> Scenario Practice: Describe how you would model the appropriate behavior for each of the following situations:
>
> 1. Scenario 1: Senior management promulgates a significant process change that your team resists.
>   - How do you demonstrate change leadership and flexibility?
> 2. Scenario 2: Two team members are in conflict, which is negatively impacting team morale.
>   - How do you model team building and conflict resolution?
> 3. Situation 3: Your department missed its quarterly target.
>   - How do you model problem-solving and accountability?
> 4. Situation 4: You receive contradictory instructions from higher management.
>   - How do you model communication and decision-making?

By emulating and acquiring these leadership actions, mid-level managers can effectively navigate the challenges of their role, guide their teams to success, and make significant contributions to overall organizational performance and growth.

> **Reflection Questions**
>
> Which situations do you find most challenging to model?
> What specific behaviors would your team observe in each situation?
> How would your modeling during these times influence team culture?

Lower-Level Management: Modeling Frontline Leadership

Lower management comprises Branch Managers, Assistant Branch Managers, and Team Leaders. These managers are directly engaged in day-to-day activities and interact closely with customers and staff, and as such, their modeling is highly visible and influential.

Day-to-Day Operations Modeling

Branch Managers exemplify overall operational leadership by managing all aspects of branch activities, including customer service, sales, and compliance. They exemplify how to meet financial goals, sustain customer satisfaction, and comply with regulatory requirements. They also exemplify community outreach and local business development.

Assistant Branch Managers provide caring leadership by assisting Branch Managers with staff management, resolving customer issues, and ensuring the smooth operation of the branch. They often specialize in leadership roles in areas such as lending, customer service, or operations.

Team Leaders provide a model for direct supervision by leading individual teams such as tellers, loan officers, or customer representatives. They set the example for how to get the team members to perform, provide excellent customer service, and meet performance goals. Team Leaders are also role models for training, development, and problem-solving.

Leadership Behaviors for Lower-Level Leaders to Emulate

Lower-level leaders have the most significant direct influence on day-to-day operations and customer experience. Their modeling behaviors have a direct impact on front-line performance and organizational reputation.

- Strong Communication: Lead by example in setting good communication by conveying information clearly to team members, attentively listening to problems, and providing clear instructions. Demonstrate how good communication ensures team alignment and efficient collaboration.
- Attention to Detail: Show exemplary attention to detail by detecting errors, adhering to

regulations, and maintaining high levels of service. Demonstrate how attention to detail prevents issues and maintains a positive organizational reputation.

- Problem-Solving: Model practical problem-solving by addressing challenges promptly and effectively, from handling customer complaints to resolving operational issues. Demonstrate thinking quickly and finding practical solutions to maintain smooth operations.

- Customer Focus: Exhibit customer-centricity by delivering positive customer experiences. Demonstrate awareness of customer needs and expectations, provide exceptional service, manage inquiries efficiently, and consistently maintain customer satisfaction.

- Leadership and Team Building: Model effective team leadership by engaging team members, creating positive working environments, and building team skills. Illustrate how effective leadership guarantees team performance and objective attainment.

- Adaptability: Set an example for flexibility by welcoming changes in regulations, technologies, and customer needs. Demonstrate how to lead teams through change with minimal disruption.

- Time Management: Demonstrate exemplary time management through prioritization of tasks, delegation of duties, and maintenance of seamless operations without any delays. Illustrate how effective time management helps in overall productivity.

Practical Activity: Frontline Modeling Plan

Step 1: Daily Modeling Opportunities (25 minutes)
Specify particular instances when you can demonstrate leadership behaviors:
- Morning Routines:
    - How do you model promptness and preparedness? What does your morning exchange with your team reveal?
- Customer Interactions:
    - How do you model customer service excellence?
    - What do your team members see when you deal with challenging customers?
- Team Meetings:
    - How do you model effective communication?
    - What leadership behaviors do you display in group settings?

- Problem-Solving Moments:
    - How do you model calm problem-solving under pressure?
    - What decision-making process are you revealing to your team?
- End-of-Day Activities:
    - How do you model reflection and continuous improvement?
    - What behaviors do you demonstrate when wrapping up work?

Step 2: Modeling Consistency Check (15 minutes)

- Do you often find yourself repeating the same behaviors in various situations?
- What behaviors are you unintentionally modeling?
- Where are the discrepancies between what you model and what you expect?

Step 3: Team Impact Evaluation (10 minutes)
Ask yourself:

- What would your team say about your modeling?
- Which of your modeled behaviors are they most likely to mimic?
- In what ways does your modeling impact team performance and culture?

By consistently demonstrating these behaviors, lower-level leaders can excel in their roles, contribute to driving organizational success, and support overall objectives, ultimately impacting customer experience and team performance.

The Modeling Cascade: How Behavior Flows Through Organizations

The influence of modeling extends not only to changing individual behavior but also to the way behaviors cascade through levels within the organization. Done well, modeling has a multiplying effect within the organization.

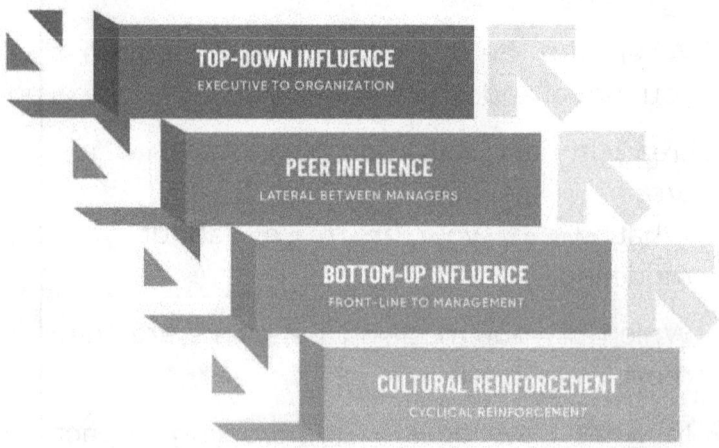

How Modeling Cascades Work

- Top-Down Influence: Executive behavior establishes the tone for the whole organization. When C-suite executives model transparency, middle managers feel authorized to be transparent. When they model innovation, it fosters risk-taking at lower levels.

- Peer Influence: Managers at the same level influence each other's behavior. When one regional manager starts having more effective meetings, others notice and alter their approach.

- Bottom-Up Influence: Excellent front-line leaders influence their managers to pay attention to the same behaviors. Exceptional customer service at the branch level can influence regional and executive agendas.

- Cultural Reinforcement: When modeling behaviors are consistent at every level, they become "how we do things here" - part of the organizational culture that reinforces itself.

Constructing Intentional Modeling Cascades
- Align behaviors across levels. Ensure that the behaviors you model reinforce the same values and goals that other levels are modeling.

- Make modeling visible. Do not just model good practice—make sure people can see and understand what you are doing and why.
- Model explicitly. Describe the behaviors you are attempting to model and request that others assist you in being consistent.
- Reward good modeling. When others demonstrate good behavior, highlight it publicly. This reinforces the behavior and sends a message to others to follow suit.

Here is an example of a successful modeling cascade. At a community bank, the CEO started every executive meeting by asking, "What did we learn this week?" This simple question modeled continuous learning and curiosity. Within three months:
- VPs began asking the same question in their department meetings
- Learning discussions were included in the regional managers' branch visits
- Branch managers started discussing learning moments in team huddles
- Front-line employees started bringing improvement ideas forward

The CEO's modeling of simplicity fostered a culture of ongoing learning, enhancing performance at all levels.

Common Modeling Errors and How to Prevent Them

Even well-intentioned leaders undermine their success with inconsistent or inappropriate modeling. Here are the most common mistakes and how to avoid them:

- The "Do as I Say, Not as I Do" Trap

    o The error: Demanding behaviors from others that you yourself don't always exhibit.

    o Example: Expecting punctuality from your staff while consistently showing up late for meetings.

    o How to avoid it: Before you expect something from others, be truthful with yourself about whether you consistently demonstrate that behavior yourself.

- The Invisible Modeling Problem

    o The mistake: Modeling good behaviors that nobody can see or understand.

    o Example: Carefully making decisions in private but coming across as indecisive to your team.

    o How to avoid it: Be more open about your good behavior by explaining your decision-making and thought process.

- The Stress Response Contradiction

- The error: Exhibiting various behaviors when stressed than under normal circumstances.
- Example: Encouraging teamwork and respectfulness, but being dictatorial in times of crises.
- How to avoid it: Practice stress management techniques and consciously maintain your modeling standards during difficult times.
- The Mixed Message Problem
  - The mistake: Modeling behavior that contradicts your stated values or priorities.
  - Example: Saying people are your priority while consistently choosing tasks over team interactions.
  - How to avoid it: Regularly audit your daily habits against your stated values and priorities.

Reflection Exercise: Consistency Modeling Check

Step 1: Values-Behavior Alignment (20 minutes)
- List your top 5 leadership values or priorities
- For every value, list three concrete behaviors that exhibit it
- Honestly assess: How frequently do you model these behaviors?

Step 2: Stress Test (15 minutes)
- Reflect on your own behavior during the most recent stressful episode
- Was your modeling congruent with your values?
- What stress behaviors arose that you would not wish your team to emulate?

Step 3: Visibility Check (10 minutes)
- Which of your positive leadership behaviors are your team likely to observe?
- What positive behaviors are you keeping to yourself?
- How can you make your finest modeling more visible?

Building Your Personal Modeling Approach

Effective modeling doesn't happen accidentally—it requires planning and consistent execution. Here's how to create your personal approach to modeling leadership:

- Step 1: Define Your Modeling Goals
    - Identify key behaviors. Based on your leadership level and organizational needs, choose 3-5 key behaviors you want to model consistently.
    - Consider your audience. Different stakeholders will need you to model different behaviors. Your boss, peers, and employees will require you to model various aspects of your leadership.
    - Be consistent with organizational culture. Ensure your modeling behaviors support the culture your organization is trying to create or maintain.
- Step 2: Plan Your Modeling Approach
    - Make it systematic. Don't leave modeling to chance. Plan specific situations where you'll intentionally model key behaviors.
    - Rehearse tough situations. Identify challenging situations in which modeling will be most difficult and rehearse your response.
    - Set reminders. Utilize calendar reminders, notes, or accountability partners to stay on track.
- Step 3: Monitor and Adjust

- Seek feedback. Regularly ask trusted colleagues about the behaviors they observe you modeling and how consistently you exhibit them.
- Self-monitor. Keep a weekly record of modeling hits and misses.

Adjust where necessary. If some behaviors are not working or are not yielding the desired results, adjust your strategy.

Personal Modeling Action Plan Template

My Leadership Level: _____

Key Behaviors I Will Model:
_____
_____
_____

Specific Situations to Model:
- Daily: _____
- Weekly: _____
- Monthly: _____
- During stress: _____

How I'll Make Modeling Visible:
_____

> _____
>
> _____
>
> Feedback Sources:
> - Who will help me check my consistency?
>
>   _____
>
> - When should I request feedback?
>
>   _____
>
> Review Schedule:
> - Weekly self-check: _____
> - Monthly assessment: _____
> - Quarterly plan update: _____

The Long-Term Effect of Continuous Modeling

As you consistently model effective leadership behaviors, the ripple effect extends far beyond your direct team. You help to create organizational culture, grow future leaders, and build lasting success.

- Cultural Impact
    - Your modeled behaviors get embedded in the organizational DNA. When leaders at all levels consistently model the same good behaviors, they create a culture that attracts top talent, retains key

employees, and achieves outstanding results.
- Leadership Development
    - Your modeling is a real-time leadership development program for all those who look up to you. Others learn leadership not only from what you say, but also from what you consistently do.
- Organizational Performance
    - Organizations that model good performance at all levels outcompete their competitors because everyone understands what good performance looks like and feels empowered to demonstrate it.
- Personal Leadership Development
    - The practice of deliberate modeling helps you become a more effective leader. As you regularly demonstrate your values and expectations, you develop more powerful leadership habits and self-awareness.

Lead People

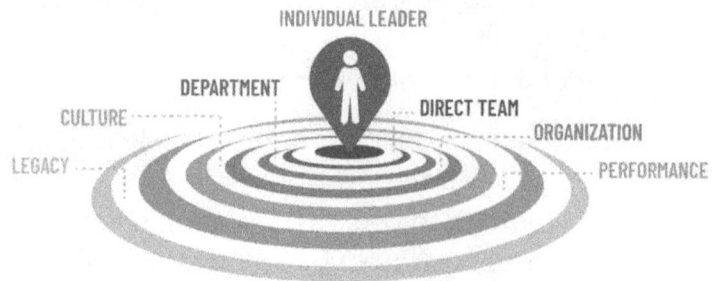

Wrapping It Up

The banking industry's clearly established management hierarchy demonstrates a fundamental leadership reality: every level of leadership serves as a model for those at lower levels. Whether you're a C-suite leader setting organizational tone, a mid-level manager translating strategy into action, or a front-line leader dealing directly with customers, your behavior constantly teaches others what leadership looks like.

Effective modeling is about being intentional, consistent, and authentic in role-modeling the behaviors you want to see throughout your organization. When you model effectively, you don't just tell people what to do; you model who to be.

Key Takeaways

- Modeling behaviors is where leadership becomes visible and real

- Different leadership levels require different modeling focus areas
- Modeling cascades through organizations, generating multiplying effects
- Being consistent between articulated values and modeled behaviors is essential
- Deliberate planning of modeling results in more effective leadership

Your Next Steps

- Complete the modeling assessment for your level of leadership
- Identify 3-5 key behaviors you want to model consistently
- Developing your own modeling action plan
- Establish feedback mechanisms to monitor your consistency
- Schedule periodic checks on your modeling efficacy

Questions for Your Team

- What leadership behaviors do you most want to see role-modeled?
- How consistently do I model the behaviors I expect of you?
- What actions have I modeled that you've attempted to imitate?

- Where do you think I have opportunities to model more?

Keep this in mind as we move forward, for our team is constantly observing and learning from your actions. Ensure that you're teaching the lessons you need them to learn through the positive example of your day-to-day actions.

In the following chapter, we will take modeling a step further. We will examine various behavioral modeling approaches and their practical applications.

PART II: STRATEGIZE

Where You're Going and How to Get There

Chapter 5

Researching and Evaluating Your Business Environment

You've established trust through your character, shown your ability through your expertise, and illustrated what leadership is all about through your everyday behavior. Now comes the strategic effort: determining where you are going and how you will get there.

However, this is where most leaders often go wrong. They dive headfirst into planning before they even understand the terrain in which they're operating. It's like trying to navigate without a map or set sail without checking the weather. You might get lucky, but you're much more likely to get lost or shipwrecked.

Researching and Evaluating Your Business Environment

Strategic leadership starts with strategic awareness. You can't map a path forward until you know the terrain you're dealing with—both the opportunities available and the challenges that might undo your efforts.

Think about it: every day, your organization is being shaped by forces you may not even be aware of. Economic trends, technological advancements, regulatory reforms, competitor movements, and customer demands are reshaping the playing field daily. Effective leaders are those who foresee these changes and position their teams to capitalize on them.

> **Reflection Question**
>
> - When was the last time you stepped back from daily operations to examine the larger picture that impacts your company?
> - What external changes have caught you off guard in the past year?

In this chapter, we will equip you with the capacity to become strategically aware, peer around corners, anticipate changes, and set your team up for success. This is not about making you a soothsayer, but about developing systematic ways to understand your environment and make better-informed strategic decisions.

Understanding Your Business Environment: The Big Picture View

Your business environment is an ecosystem—a sophisticated network of interdependent forces that shape how your organization works, competes, and thrives. Just as a seasoned captain reads wind patterns, weather systems, and ocean currents before charting a course, good leaders learn to read the patterns of their business environment.

There are two significant parts of the business environment that you should learn about:

- Macro-Environment: These are the large, general forces that influence not only your organization, but your whole industry and economy. Consider these as the weather patterns that everyone must contend with—economic conditions, political trends, social trends, technological innovation, environmental issues, and legal reforms.

- Micro-Environment: These are the forces more closely associated with your particular organization and industry. These are your customers, suppliers, competitors, distributors, and other stakeholders that directly influence your day-to-day operations.

It is crucial to understand both levels since they influence one another in a way that generates both threats and opportunities for your organization.

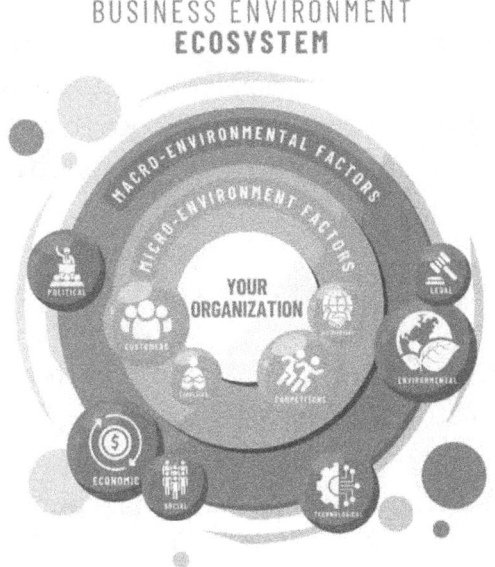

Why Environmental Analysis Matters

Allow me to illustrate with a real-life example of why it is essential. In 2007, the majority of conventional bookstore executives were preoccupied with the immediate surroundings—streamlining store formats, managing inventory, and competing with other bookstores. But they overlooked the macro-environmental revolution occurring around them: the intersection of internet technology, shifting reading patterns, and new business models.

Amazon was not only another bookstore competitor, but it also signified a paradigm shift in the way individuals would consume and purchase books. Those leaders who recognized this environmental shift early on either changed their strategies or aligned themselves with digital platforms. Those that did not? The majority of their stores are now closed down.

This type of environmental myopia occurs in all sectors. The executives who succeed are those who build systematic methods for scanning the environment, recognizing emerging patterns, and adapting their strategies accordingly.

The PESTEL Framework: Scanning the Macro-Environment

PESTEL analysis is your formal way of analyzing the macro-environmental forces that may influence your organization. It is like your early warning system for substantial changes that may impact your strategy.

PESTEL stands for Political, Economic, Social, Technological, Environmental, and Legal factors. These are the primary sectors where trends and indicators exist that will inform future changes. A PESTEL analysis is more than just an academic exercise—it's a practical intelligence-gathering tool to help make better-informed decisions.

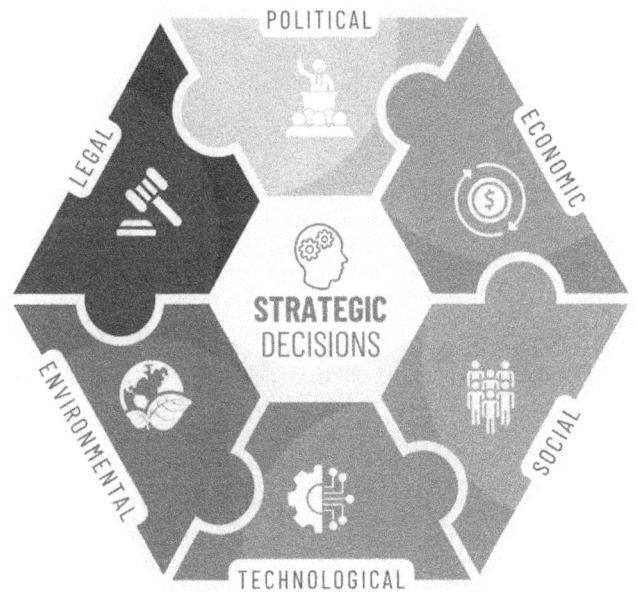

PESTEL ANALYSIS FRAMEWORK

Political Factors: The Rules of the Game

Political considerations encompass government policies, regulations, political stability, and international relations that may impact your company. These are not merely esoteric policy debates—they have actual implications for how you can do business.

What to watch for:
- Tax law changes that can affect your costs or consumer spending
- Regulatory reform that may affect your business
- Priorities in government spending that might create opportunities
- Trade policies that could affect your supply chain or access to markets
- Political stability, which influences business confidence

Real-world application: If you are in the healthcare field, suggested modifications to healthcare policy are not merely political headlines—they're strategic information that may inherently change your operating landscape. If you are in manufacturing, shifts in trade policy may influence your cost structure and competitive situation.

Economic Factors: The Financial Weather

Economic characteristics include the monetary conditions that affect purchasing power, spending habits, and business expenses. Keeping up with financial trends enables you to forecast shifts in demand and make necessary adjustments in your strategies.

Key areas to watch:
- Interest rates and their implications for borrowing costs and customer spending
- Inflationary pressures affecting your cost and pricing strategies
- Employment rates affect consumer expenditures and labor availability
- Patterns of economic trends indicating market expansion or contraction
- Fluctuations in currency are impacting global operations

Real-world example: If economic indicators signal that a recession is imminent, this should enter into your strategic decisions. You may want to focus on cash management, defer significant capital investments, or shift your product line to lower-priced offerings.

Social Factors: Knowing Your Evolving Market

Social factors encompass demographic trends, cultural shifts, lifestyle adjustments, and shifts in consumer attitudes. These trends often develop slowly but can have a profound impact on your market in the long term.

Key trends to watch:
- Demographic shifts in your customer base

- Shifting lifestyle preferences are affecting product demand
- Cultural attitudes towards your products or industry
- Education levels influencing skill availability and customer sophistication
- Health and environmental concerns are influencing consumer purchasing habits

Strategic implication: Increasingly, the emphasis on sustainability is not a fad, but a fundamental shift in consumer values that can create new market opportunities and challenge traditional business models. Early movers can get ahead.

Technological Factors: The Innovation Environment

Technological forces entail developments and innovations in technology that might bring opportunities or threats to your company. In today's rapidly changing world, being technologically aware is crucial for success and survival.

Areas of concentration:
- Automation technologies that might transform your operations
- Digital platforms that could disrupt your industry

- Data analytics competencies that would result in competitive advantages
- Communication technologies that may alter customer expectations
- Emerging technologies that could create new business models

You don't need to be a tech specialist, but you do need to understand how technological changes could affect your business model, customers' expectations, and competitive landscape.

Environmental Factors: Sustainability and Resource Concerns

Environmental factors encompass ecological conditions, including climate change, sustainability issues, and the availability of resources. These are becoming increasingly significant as companies face pressure to conduct their business in a responsible manner.

Key considerations:
- Environmental regulations on operations
- Sustainability requirements of customers and stakeholders
- Impacts of climate change on operations and supply chains

- Resource scarcity is impacting costs and availability
- Environmental opportunities for new products or services

Legal Factors: The Compliance Environment

Legal factors involve your company's laws, regulations, and the legal system in which it operates. Staying ahead of the law helps you avoid compliance issues and enables you to identify new opportunities for growth.

Key areas:
- Industry-specific rules governing operations
- Employment laws affecting HR practices
- Consumer protection law affecting product design
- Intellectual property rights affecting innovation
- International laws that influence global operations

Practical Activity: Vision Development Exercise

Step 1: Information Gathering (30 minutes)
For each PESTEL factor, identify 2-3 current trends or changes that could affect your organization:

- Political:

_____

_____

_____

- Economic:

_____

_____

_____

- Social:

_____

_____

_____

- Technological:

_____

_____

- Environmental:

  _____
  _____
  _____

- Legal:

  _____
  _____
  _____

Step 2: Impact Assessment (20 minutes)
For each trend, evaluate:
- Impact Level: High, Medium, or Low
- Timeline: When will this affect us? (Next 6 months, 1 year, 2+
- years)
- Opportunity or Threat: Could this help or hurt us?

Step 3: Strategic Implications (10 minutes)
- What three trends do you think would have the most significant effect on your strategy?

- What should you be monitoring more closely?
- What actions should you consider taking now?

Porter's Five Forces: Knowing Your Competitive Environment

Whereas PESTEL makes you learn about the general environment, Porter's Five Forces is interested in your competitive environment—the forces that shape how attractive and profitable your industry is, and where the actual competitive pressures originate.

Consider this as your competitive intelligence system. It enables you to see not only who your competitors are, but also where competitive pressure originates and how you can best position yourself to respond.

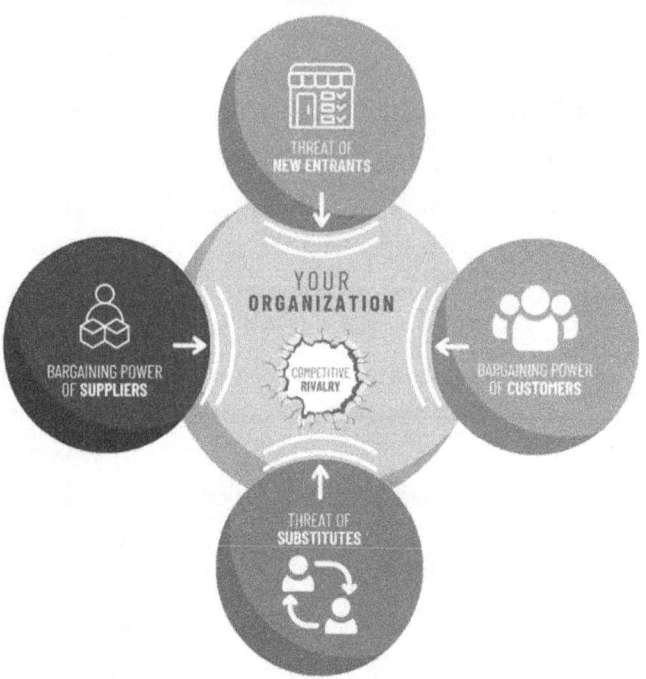

Threat of New Entrants: Who Might Join the Party?

This force examines how easy or difficult it is for new rivals to enter your market. High entry barriers shield current players; low entry barriers signal that you must be continually concerned about new competition.

Major issues to consider:
- Capital requirements: How much does it cost to start up in your business?
- Economies of scale: Do big players have significant cost advantages?
- Brand loyalty: How committed are the customers to existing providers?
- Access to distribution channels: How easy is it for new entrants to reach the customers?
- Government regulations: Do regulatory or licensing requirements pose barriers?
- Technology needs: Does it need specialized technology or knowledge?

Strategic questions to ask:
- What would it take for our market to get a new entrant?
- What barriers currently protect us from new entrants?
- How can we strengthen those barriers?
- Which new entrants should we be looking out for?

Real-world example: The taxi business had decades of high barriers to entry—costly medallions, regulatory hurdles, and local knowledge requirements. Then, Uber and Lyft leveraged technology to bypass these traditional barriers, fundamentally transforming the competitive landscape.

Bargaining Power of Suppliers: Who Controls Your Inputs?

This examines the extent to which your suppliers have leverage over you. Powerful suppliers can squeeze your margins by raising prices or reducing quality, while weak suppliers give you more control over costs and terms.

Factors that heighten supplier power:
- There are limited suppliers for key inputs.
- High switching costs to change suppliers
- Suppliers' products are highly differentiated
- Suppliers can forward-integrate into your business
- Your company is not an ideal customer for suppliers

Strategic considerations:
- Which suppliers could significantly impact our operations if they were to increase prices or reduce service levels?

- How might we decrease our reliance on powerful suppliers?
- Which alternative sources or suppliers of inputs should we develop?
- Could we integrate backward to control key inputs ourselves?

Bargaining Power of Customers: Who Controls Your Revenue?

Customer power controls the degree to which your customers can influence pricing, quality, and service levels. Strong customers will insist on lower prices, better quality, and improved service, compressing your profitability.

Factors that enhance customer power:
- Large customers who buy in bulk
- Standardized products with numerous substitute suppliers
- Low switching costs for customers
- Customers have adequate information on substitutes. Customers may backward integrate into your company.

Key questions:

- Who are the customers with the most significant leverage on our prices and terms?
- How concentrated is our customer base?
- What would it cost customers to switch to competitors?
- How could we increase switching costs for customers or reduce their bargaining power?

Threat of Substitutes: What Else Could Customers Do?

Substitutes are not only direct competitors—they are alternatives that customers might use to fulfill the same need. The threat of substitutes limits your pricing and profitability ceiling.

Examples of substitute threats:
- Email substituting for postal mail
- Video conferencing is replacing business travel
- Streaming services replacing cable television
- Mobile payments replacing cash and cards

Analysis framework:
- In what other ways could customers fulfill the same need?
- How does the substitutes' price-performance ratio compare to that of our product?

- What trends would make substitutes more appealing?
- How could we make alternatives less appealing or make changing more difficult?

Competitive Rivalry: The Struggle for Market Share

This force examines the intensity of competition among existing competitors. Fierce competition often leads to price wars, increased marketing expenses, and pressure on profitability.

Factors that enhance rivalry:
- Several competitors of a similar size
- Slow industry growth is forcing companies to steal share
- High fixed expenses exerting pressure to keep volume
- Insufficient product differentiation resulting in price competition
- High exit barriers trap poorly performing competitors in the industry

Strategic implications:
- How competitive is pricing in our industry?
- On what basis can we compete other than price?

- How could we differentiate our offering to reduce direct competition?
- What would it take to attain sustainable competitive advantage?

Interactive Exercise: Five Forces Evaluation

Step 1: Force Evaluation (25 minutes)
Rate each force as High, Medium, or Low threat/power:
- Threat of New Entrants: _____
    - What barriers currently protect your market?
    - What would reduce these barriers?
- Supplier Power: _____
    - Which suppliers have the most leverage over you?
    - What are the alternatives you have?
- Customer Power: _____
    - Who are the most influential customers?
    - How easily could they switch to competitors?
- Threat of Substitutes: _____
    - What alternatives could replace your product/service?
    - How attractive are these alternatives becoming?
- Competitive Rivalry: _____
    - How competitive is your industry?
    - What's the basis of competition (price, quality, service, etc.)?

> Step 2: Strategic Insights (15 minutes)
> - What forces pose the most significant challenges for your organization?
> - What is your most significant competitive advantage?
> - What strategic moves could improve your position?
>
> Step 3: Action Planning (10 minutes)
> - What will you monitor more closely based on this analysis?
> - What strategic initiatives should you consider?
> - How will you track changes in these competitive forces?

SWOT Analysis: Linking Internal Capabilities with External Realities

Now that you know your external environment via PESTEL and Five Forces analysis, it's time to link that intelligence to a candid evaluation of your internal capabilities. SWOT analysis—looking at your Strengths, Weaknesses, Opportunities, and Threats—allows you to view how well you are positioned to thrive in your environment.

Yet, here's what most leaders do wrong with SWOT analysis: they use it as a brainstorming activity rather than a strategic planning tool. The actual value of SWOT analysis lies in matching your internal situation with your external context to develop targeted strategic actions.

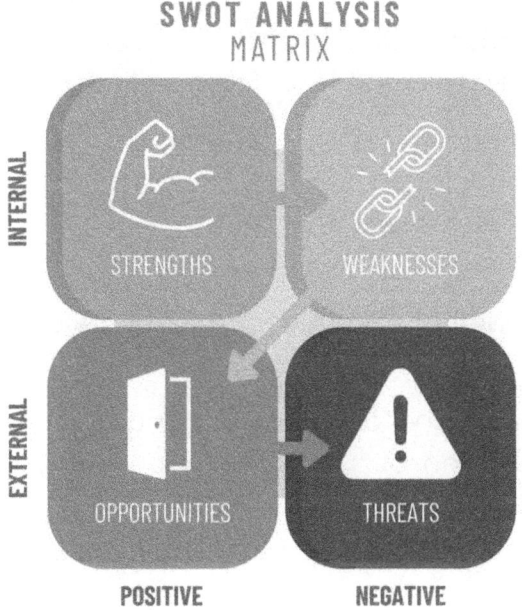

Strengths: What You Do Well

Strengths are internal skills that give you an edge over others. But don't just list what you think you're good at—focus on strengths that actually have practical importance in your competitive context.

Types of organizational strengths:

- Operational strengths: Improved processes, cost advantages, quality systems
- Market strengths: Market position, customer loyalty, strong brand identification
- Financial strengths: Low debt, high cash flow, access to capital
- Human capital strengths: Organizational culture, strong leadership, skilled workforce
- Technological strengths: Proprietary technology, data capabilities, digital infrastructure
- Strategic strengths: Close alliances, distinctive market position, economies of scale

Critical questions to determine genuine strengths:
- What do our customers constantly praise us for?
- What do we do more effectively than any rival?
- Which internal capabilities propel our greatest successes?
- What are the benefits that competitors would find hard to match?

Weaknesses: Areas Where You Must Improve

Weaknesses are internal deficiencies that put you at a disadvantage. The key is being brutally honest about where you are weak so that you can remediate them or avoid strategies that would expose these weaknesses.

Typical organizational weaknesses:
- Operational weaknesses: Inefficient processes, high costs, quality problems
- Market weaknesses: Weak brand identification, limited market exposure, and concentration of customers
- Financial weaknesses: Cash flow problems, high indebtedness, limited resources
- Human capital weaknesses: Skills gaps, negative culture, leadership limitations
- Technological weaknesses: Outdated systems, limited digital capabilities
- Strategic weaknesses: Excessive reliance on key relationships, insufficient diversification

Critical questions for finding weakness:
- What do the customers constantly complain about?
- Where do the competitors outperform us consistently?
- What internal constraints limit our performance?

- What are the missing capabilities we require for success in the future?

Opportunities: External Possibilities

Opportunities are the external drivers that you may be in a position to exploit for advantage. These emerge from the developments in your PESTEL and competitive landscape, creating new possibilities for growth or improvement.

Sources of opportunities:
- Market opportunities: Emerging segments, unserved markets, shifting customer requirements
- Technology opportunities: Possibilities of automation, digitalization, and new functionality
- Competitive opportunities: Competitors' weaknesses, industry consolidation, new alliances
- Regulatory opportunities: Favorable policy changes, deregulation, new legislation
- Economic opportunities: Economic growth, low interest rates, and a reduction in costs
- Social opportunities: Demographic trends, lifestyle changes, value shifts

Opportunity identification questions:
- What environmental trends would be suitable for our business?
- Which new customer groups or markets might we serve?
- What competitor weaknesses could we exploit?
- What emerging technologies could offer benefits?

Threats: External Threats

Threats are external factors that could damage your organization. Identifying threats early allows you to prepare defenses or alter course to avoid them entirely.

Common threat categories:
- Competitive threats: New entrants, aggressive competitors, disruptive business models
- Market threats: Decreasing demand, loss of customers, substitute goods
- Technology threats: Obsolescence dangers, cybersecurity threats, and disruptive innovations
- Regulatory threats: Upcoming regulations, compliance costs, legal battles
- Economic threats: Inflation, recession, currency instability, disruption of supplies

- Social threats: Shifting tastes, demographic change, reputational risks

Threat analysis questions:
- What changes in our environment could hurt our business?
- What are our most significant vulnerabilities to external changes?
- What if our key assumptions about the future were wrong?
- What are our rivals up to that might endanger our standing?

Connecting SWOT to Strategy

The real power of SWOT analysis comes from matching the four quadrants to establish specific strategic initiatives:
- SO Strategies (Strength-Opportunity): In what ways are you able to utilize your strengths to capitalize on opportunities?
    - Example: If you have strong customer relationships (strength) and there's growing demand for sustainable products (opportunity), you could leverage those relationships to introduce eco-friendly offerings.

- WO Strategies (Weakness-Opportunity): How can you overcome weaknesses to pursue opportunities?
  - Example: If you have no digital capabilities (weakness) but there is an opportunity in e-commerce (opportunity), you may need to invest in technology or collaborate with digital specialists.
- ST Strategies (Strength-Threat): How can you use your strengths to defend against threats?
  - Example: If you possess robust cash reserves (strength) and an economic downturn endangers your market (threat), you might utilize your financial strength to invest in market share or purchase struggling competitors.
- WT Strategies (Weakness-Threat): In what ways can you reduce weaknesses and evade threats?
  - Example: If you have limited technical expertise (weakness) and are vulnerable to cybersecurity attacks (threat), you might outsource IT security or invest heavily in cybersecurity training.

Interactive Exercise: SWOT Analysis Worksheet

Step 1: Internal Analysis (20 minutes)
Strengths (What are our advantages?)

1._____

2._____

3._____

4._____

5._____

Weaknesses (Where Do We Need Improvement?)

1._____

2._____

3._____

4._____

5._____

Step 2: External Analysis (20 minutes)
Opportunities (What external factors could benefit us?)

1._____

2._____

3._____

4._____

5._____

Threats (What external factors can hurt us?)
1._____

2._____

3._____

4._____

5._____

Step 3: Strategic Action Development (20 minutes)

SO Strategies (Use strengths to pursue opportunities):

```
┌─────────────────────────────────────────────┐
│  _____ │
│                                              │
│  WO Strategies (Overcome weaknesses to pursue│
│  opportunities):                             │
│  _____ │
│                                              │
│  ST Strategies (Use strengths to defend against│
│  threats):                                   │
│  _____ │
│                                              │
│   WT Strategies (Minimize weaknesses and avoid│
│  threats):                                   │
│  _____ │
└─────────────────────────────────────────────┘
```

Market Research and Competitive Intelligence: Staying Informed

Learning about your environment is not a single exercise, but a continuous one needing systematic information collection and analysis. Those leaders who consistently make sound strategic choices possess superior information about their environment.

Primary Research: Collecting Information First-Hand

Primary research involves collecting firsthand information by directly contacting customers, competitors, suppliers, and other stakeholders. This provides you with information specific to your needs and circumstances.

Customer research methods:
- Surveys and questionnaires: Organized data collection from large customer numbers
- Interviews: Rich, qualitative information from individual customers
- Focus groups: Group discussions that reveal customer preferences and attitudes
- Observation: Observing customers' actual behavior as opposed to what they tell you
- Beta testing: Obtaining feedback from customers on new products or services prior to full launch

Competitive intelligence gathering:
- Industry conferences and events: Networking and information sharing opportunities
- Customer feedback: What customers say about competitors
- Supplier intelligence: Feedback from standard suppliers regarding competitors' moves
- Public information: Annual reports, press releases, website analysis, social media monitoring

- Mystery shopping: Firsthand experience of competitor offerings

Secondary Research: Leveraging Existing Information

Secondary research involves analysis of existing data from industry reports, market studies, government statistics, and academic research. This provides a broader context and industry benchmarks.

Informative secondary sources:
- Industry associations: Industry statistics, industry reports, trade magazines
- Government sources: Economic statistics, regulatory data, demographic data
- Financial reports: Public company filings, analyst reports, market research
- Academic research: University studies, business school case studies
- Media sources: Trend analysis, expert commentary, industry news

Building Your Intelligence System

The challenge lies in creating organized processes for gathering, analyzing, and distributing environmental intelligence within your business.

Intelligence collection framework:

- Assign responsibility: Who will oversee the various aspects of your environment?

- Establish sources: What publications, websites, reports, and contacts will you monitor regularly?

- Establish sharing mechanisms: How will you share insights throughout your organization?

- Schedule reviews: At what point will you formally assess environmental changes and their implications?

- Relate to decisions: In what ways will environmental intelligence impact your strategic planning process?

Stakeholder Mapping and Engagement

Your business environment is not made up of abstract forces alone—it is populated with actual people and institutions that have interests in your success or failure. Knowing and dealing with such stakeholders is of importance for environmental awareness and strategic success.

Identifying Your Stakeholders

Internal stakeholders:
- Management teams and staff
- Board of directors and owners
- Labor unions (if any)

Direct external stakeholders:

- Customers and customer segments
- Suppliers and business partners
- Investors and lenders
- Distributors and channel partners

Indirect external stakeholders:
- Government departments and regulatory bodies
- Industry associations and standard-setting organizations
- Media and industry pundits
- Local communities and activist organizations
- Competitors (who influence your universe, although you might not directly deal with them)

Stakeholder Analysis Framework

For each stakeholder group, you should be aware of:
- Interest level: To what extent are they interested in your organization and its work?
- Influence level: To what extent do they have the power to influence your success?
- Current relationship: Are they supportive, neutral, or against your objectives?

- Information needs: What do they need to know from you?
- Communication preferences: How do they wish to get information and provide feedback?

Step 1: Stakeholder Identification (15 minutes)
List your key stakeholders in each category:

High Influence, High Interest (Manage closely):

_____

_____

_____

High Influence, Low Interest (Keep satisfied):

_____

_____

_____

Low Influence, High Interest (Stay informed):

_____

_____

_____

Low Influence, Low Interest (Monitor):

_____

_____

_____

Step 2: Engagement Strategy (20 minutes)
For each high-influence stakeholder, define:
- o   Current relationship status
- o   What information do they need from you
- o   How often should you communicate with them
- o   Most effective means of communication
- o   How they might assist with environmental intelligence

Step 3: Intelligence Opportunities (10 minutes)
- o   Who are the stakeholders that might offer useful environmental information?
- o   What questions should you ask them about trends and changes?
- o   How do you formalize gathering intelligence from stakeholders?

Stakeholder Engagement Strategies

For high-influence, high-interest stakeholders (manage closely):
- Regular, direct communication
- Involve them in planning activities as required
- Seek their input on strategic decisions
- Provide thorough progress and setback updates

For high-influence, low-interest stakeholders (keep satisfied):
- Periodic revisions of essential developments
- Ensure their needs are met without overwhelming them with details
- Be responsive when they do engage
- Monitor for changes in their interest level

For high-interest, low-influence stakeholders (keep informed):
- Regular communication through newsletters, updates, or meetings
- Give open information regarding your activities
- Offer opportunities for feedback and input
- Utilize them as advocates whenever necessary

For low-interest, low-influence stakeholders (monitor):
- Limited but polite interaction
- Monitor for changes in their situation that might increase their influence or interest.
- Be prepared to adjust the interaction if their condition changes.

Systematic Environmental Monitoring: Making It Operational

Learning about your surroundings should not be a one-time strategic planning exercise. The best leaders make environmental scanning a part of their regular operating habits.

Developing Your Environmental Scanning System

Daily checking routine:
- Read industry news and magazines
- Monitor key competitor actions
- Monitor applicable economic indicators
- Stay current on regulatory developments

Weekly analysis steps:
- Collect and share environmental information with your employees
- Evaluate how environmental shifts could impact ongoing projects

- Update stakeholder intelligence
- Re-evaluate and revise monitoring priorities

Monthly strategic reviews:
- Formal environmental assessment meetings
- Update PESTEL, Five Forces, and SWOT analyses
- Assess the strategic implications of environmental shifts
- Adjust strategic plans based on new intelligence

Quarterly strategic planning:
- In-depth environmental examination
- Stakeholder feedback incorporation
- Strategic plan updates
- Environmental intelligence training for members

> **Interactive Exercise: Environmental Scanning Checklist**
>
> Daily Intelligence Collection:
> - Review of industry news (15 minutes)
> - Competitor monitoring (10 minutes)
> - Economic indicator check (5 minutes)
> - Regulatory update scan (5 minutes)
>
> Weekly Analysis:
> - Compile weekly intelligence summary
> - Share insights with the team
> - Update stakeholder intelligence
> - Assess the impact on current initiatives
>
> Monthly Strategic Review:
> - Formal environmental assessment meeting
> - Update PESTEL analysis
> - Update Five Forces analysis
> - Revise SWOT analysis
> - Evaluate strategic implications
>
> Quarterly Planning Integration:

- Detailed environmental review
- Stakeholder feedback incorporation
- Strategic plan changes
- Team environmental intelligence training

Key Sources to Monitor:
    Industry Publications: _____

    Government Sources: _____

    Competitor Information: _____

    Economic Indicators: _____

    Technology Trends: _____

    Regulatory Sources: _____

Making Environmental Intelligence Actionable

The goal is not just to gather data—it's to translate environmental intelligence into better-informed strategic decisions.

Here is how you can render your environmental analysis actionable:
- Connect intelligence to decision-making: In all major strategic decisions, explicitly consider

relevant environmental factors and their potential impact on outcomes.

- Scenario planning: Utilize environmental intelligence to develop multiple scenarios for how your environment might evolve, and have strategies in place for each.

- Early warning systems: Identify key indicators that would typify significant environmental changes, and regularly track these indicators.

- Strategic flexibility: Incorporate adaptability into your plans to enable quick adjustments when environmental conditions change.

- Team training: Educate your team on how environmental forces impact your company so they can assist in intelligence gathering and strategic thought.

Interactive Exercise

Step 1: Opportunity Identification (20 minutes)

Based on your environmental analysis, identify potential opportunities:

    Market Opportunities:
___

    New customer segments:
___

    Unmet customer needs:
___

    Geographic expansion:
___

    Technology Opportunities:
    Process improvements:
___

    New product capabilities:
___

    Digital transformation:
___

    Competitive Opportunities:
    Competitor weaknesses:
___

    Market gaps:
___

Partnership opportunities:
_____

Step 2: Opportunity Evaluation (15 minutes)

For each opportunity, assess:
- Size: How big can this opportunity possibly be? (Small/Medium/Large)
- Fit: How well does this align with our capabilities? (Poor/Good/Excellent)
- Timeline: When should we pursue this? (Now/6 months/1+ years)
- Competition: How many others are likely to pursue this?

Step 3: Setting Priorities (10 minutes)
- Which 3 opportunities should you investigate further?
- What additional information do you need about these opportunities?
- Who could help you evaluate these opportunities?
- What would be the first step to pursue each opportunity?

Developing Your Environmental Intelligence Capability

Becoming strategically aware does not occur overnight—it is an ability that you develop over time. The most effective leaders create systems and habits that make environmental intelligence a natural component of their leadership approach.

Developing Your Personal Intelligence Network

- Industry contacts: Establish connections with individuals who can provide valuable insights into industry trends, competitors' moves, and market evolution.

- Customer relationships: Maintain direct contact with key customers who can provide early indications of evolving needs and preferences.

- Supplier alliances: Cultivate relationships with suppliers that can provide insight into overall market conditions and competitor movements.

- Expert advisors: Connect with consultants, analysts, and professors who specialize in your business or functional areas.

- Cross-industry learning: Find counterparts in other industries who face similar issues and can provide fresh perspectives.

Investment in Intelligence Capabilities

- Information systems: Invest in systems and tools that enable you to collect, organize, and analyze environmental information more efficiently and effectively.

- Team development: Train team members to collect and assess environmental intelligence as part of their ongoing job responsibilities.

- External sources: Consider hiring consultants, subscribing to expert research services, or joining industry intelligence-sharing associations.

- Technology tools: Utilize business intelligence software, social media monitoring tools, and data analytics capabilities to enhance your environmental scanning capabilities.

Developing a Learning Organization

The finest environmental intelligence is achieved in organizations where all members participate in learning about the environment. Develop systems that promote and reward environmental consciousness within your organization:

- Intelligence sharing sessions: Regular forums where team members share environmental observations and implications.

- Customer contact rotation: Ensure multiple team members have direct customer contact and can gather market intelligence.

- Cross-functional teams: Create teams that span different functions and can provide diverse perspectives on environmental changes.

- External Learning Opportunities: Encourage team members to attend industry events, participate in trade associations, and establish external networks.

Common Environmental Analysis Mistakes to Avoid

Even well-meaning leaders can sabotage their own environmental analysis. The following are the most frequent pitfalls and how to circumvent them:

The Echo Chamber Trap

- The error: Only seeking information from sources that reinforce what you already think or want to hear.

- Why it happens: It is only natural to give greater attention to information that reinforces our current opinions and to downplay information that contradicts them.

- How to prevent it: Actively seek out alternative perspectives, including those of people who do not share your current thinking. Assign team members to serve as "devil's advocates" for environmental scanning.

The Analysis Paralysis Problem

- The error: Collecting so much environmental data that you become confused and cannot make decisions.

- Why it happens: Environmental scanning can be addictive—there is always more information you could gather and analyze.

- How to avoid it: Set clear limits on information gathering, focus on actionable intelligence, and set decision-making time limits for yourself that force you to act on the available information.

The Internal Focus Bias

- The error: Devoting excessive time to the examination of internal capabilities and insufficient time to comprehending external environment alterations.

- Why it happens: Internal information is more accessible and easier to analyze than external information, so leaders tend to rely on what they can manage.

- How to avoid it: Allocate specific time and resources to external environmental scanning, and hold yourself accountable for staying externally focused.

The Static Thinking Error

- The mistake: Treating environmental analysis as one exercise rather than an ongoing process.
- Why it happens: Strategic planning is conducted on an annual cycle, so leaders assume environmental analysis is also a yearly process.
- How to prevent it: Incorporate environmental monitoring into your day-to-day management processes, and revise your environmental scan on an ongoing basis as new data emerges.

The Prediction Trap

- The mistake: Trying to predict exactly what will happen in your environment rather than preparing for multiple possibilities.
- Why it happens: Leaders feel compelled to provide certainty about the future and consequently make overconfident estimates based on incomplete data.
- How to avoid it: Concentrate on developing potential scenarios and creating flexibility in

your plans, rather than attempting to foresee precisely what will occur.

Practical Activity: Monthly Environmental Review Template

Date: _____

Reviewer: _____

Key Environmental Changes This Month:

Political/Regulatory:

_____

_____

Economic:

_____

_____

Social/Cultural:

_____

_____

Technological:

_____

_____

Strategic Implications:

- What opportunities have emerged?
  _____

- What new threats have appeared?
  _____

- What do we need to modify in our strategy?
  _____

- What further intelligence do we require?
  _____

Action Items:
_____
_____
_____

Areas of Focus for Next Month:
_____
_____

Wrapping It Up

Strategic leadership starts with strategic awareness. You cannot chart a successful course if you are not aware of the context in which you are working. The frameworks and tools in this chapter (PESTEL analysis, Porter's Five Forces, SWOT analysis, stakeholder mapping, and systematic environmental monitoring) provide you with the ability to anticipate changes before they catch you off guard.

Yet keep this in mind: it's not about turning yourself into a flawless forecaster of the future. It's about being increasingly attentive to the forces that influence your world, so you can make more informed strategic choices and set your organization up for success, no matter what the future may bring.

The executives who consistently outcompete their rivals are brilliant, to be sure. Still, they're also better informed about the world around them and more methodical in leveraging that information to make decisions.

Environmental intelligence should inform your daily leadership decisions. When you understand the broader context in which your organization operates, you make better choices about resource allocation, risk management, and opportunity pursuit.

Key Takeaways

- Strategic awareness comes before strategic success: you cannot formulate good strategies without knowing your environment
- Use systematic frameworks: PESTEL, Five Forces, and SWOT provide structured approaches to environmental analysis

- Environmental monitoring ought to be a continuous exercise and not a once-a-year activity
- Link intelligence to action: The objective is improved decisions, not necessarily improved information
- Build organizational capability: The best environmental intelligence comes from organizations where everyone contributes to environmental awareness

Your Next Steps

- Finish the environmental analysis activities in this chapter for your company
- Establish systematic monitoring routines using the checklists and templates provided
- Develop your intelligence network by determining principal sources and contacts for environmental information
- Conduct routine environmental assessments to make this a continuing capability
- Train your staff on environmental analysis so that all contribute to strategic awareness

Questions for Your Team

- What environmental changes have we previously overlooked that negatively impact our performance?
- Which sources of environmental intelligence ought we to be tracking more systematically? How can we more effectively incorporate ecological consciousness into our everyday decision-making?
- What outside relationships do we need to develop to enhance our environmental intelligence?

The last part of strategic leadership is to turn your environmental intelligence into a concrete strategic plan. In Chapter 6, we'll walk through the step-by-step process of strategic planning—how to take everything you've learned about your environment and turn it into a roadmap for success. Environmental awareness provides the raw material for strategy. Let's now find out how to shape that raw material into a strategic plan that works.

Chapter 6

Writing Your Strategic Plan

You've done your homework. You understand your environment, you've studied your competitive position, and you have a solid sense of your organization's strengths and weaknesses. Now comes the step where most leaders stumble: translating all that analysis into an actual plan that really guides decision-making and drives results.

Most strategic plans are impressive to view in PowerPoint presentations, but they often struggle to withstand the harsh realities of the world. They're full of lofty vision statements and challenging goals, but they lack practical details to inform day-to-day decisions. They end up as dusty documents on shelves instead of tools to catalyze action.

Excellent strategic planning prioritizes creating a helpful map over creating the perfect document, one that guides you and your team in making better daily decisions. It's about creating alignment around where you're going and how you're going to get there. It's about building accountability mechanisms that ensure your strategy is actually executed.

In this chapter, we will walk you through the step-by-step, practical process of developing an effective strategic plan that operates in the real world. You will learn how to convert your environmental analysis into specific strategic decisions, how to set goals that truly influence behavior, and how to establish the systems that will translate strategy into results.

Reflection Question

Think about strategic plans you've been involved with in the past.
- What made the difference between plans that actually influenced behavior and decisions versus those that just gathered dust?
- What practical aspects were lacking in the unsuccessful plans?

The Foundation: Mission, Vision, and Values That Really Matter

Every strategic plan begins with a clear mission, vision, and values. And this is where most companies get it wrong: they treat these as marketing slogans rather than strategic tools. They create mission statements that sound wonderful but don't actually guide decisions. They devise visions that are inspiring but impossibly vague. They delineate values that nobody can disagree with, but that won't offer any direction when tough decisions need to be made.

Your mission, vision, and values should serve as strategic tools that help you make informed decisions, allocate resources effectively, and stay focused. If they're not helping you say "no" to the unimportant so you can say "yes" to the important, they're not doing their job.

Mission: Your Reason for Being

Your mission answers the fundamental question: Why does our organization exist beyond making money? It should be specific enough to guide decision-making but broad enough to allow for growth and adaptation.

Characteristics of a good mission:
- Specific to what you do: Generalities like "providing excellent service" fail to help anyone make a clear strategic decision
- Be clear about whom you serve: You cannot serve everyone equally well
- Focused on impact: What difference do you make in the world?
- Memorable and actionable: If individuals cannot remember it, they cannot use it to inform decisions

Testing your mission statement:
- Does it assist in making choices about which opportunities to take and which to decline?
- Can new employees determine what is expected of them?
- Does it differentiate you from the competition in meaningful ways?
- Would you make different decisions if you had a different mission?

Vision: Your Image of Success

Your vision defines what future success is. It must be difficult enough to encourage effort but clear enough that individuals can understand what you're working toward.

Components of clear vision:
- Time-bound: Typically 3-5 years away, specific enough to be attainable
- Measurable: You should be able to determine if you've reached it
- Inspirational: It must inspire people to strive for it
- Realistic: Ambitious yet not delusional

Vision development process:
- Start with current reality: Where are you now?
- Identify key trends: What changes will shape your future environment?
- Leverage strengths: In what ways can you capitalize on what you do best?
- Address challenges: What obstacles must you overcome?
- Paint the picture: What would success be in concrete, measurable terms?

VISION DEVELOPMENT PROCESS

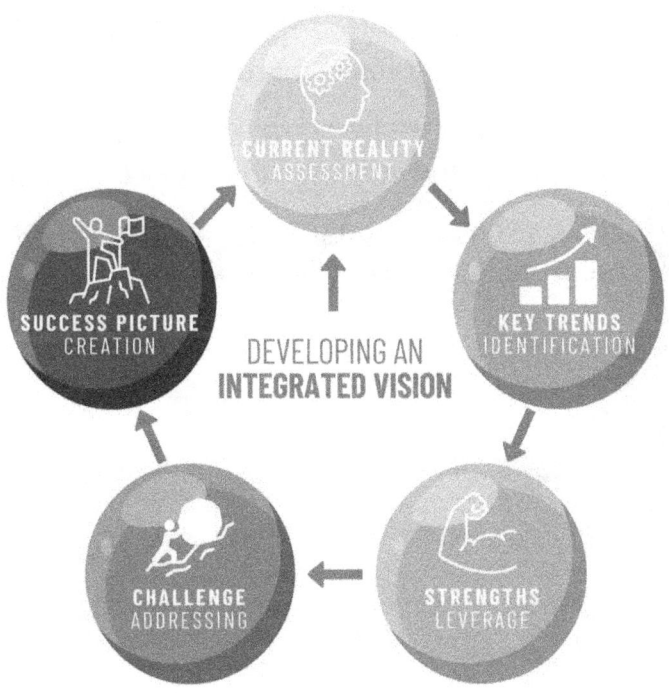

Values: Your Decision-Making Principles

Values are the morals that guide the way you operate. They should help you make tough decisions when different stakeholders have conflicting interests or when you face moral dilemmas.

Features of actionable values:

- Specific enough to guide decisions: "Integrity" is too vague; while "We tell customers the truth even if it loses us sales" is specific
- Sparse in number: You can't have 12 core values; identify 3-5 that really matter
- Consistently practiced: When you make exceptions, they're not values, really
- Measurable: You ought to be in a position to measure if you're fulfilling them

Practical Activity: Mission, Vision, Values Development Workshop

Step 1: Clarification of Mission (30 minutes)
Answer these questions:
- What is it that we do that is of value to others?
- Whom precisely do we serve?
- In what way are we different from other firms that serve the same customers?
- What would be lost if our organization were to disappear?
- Draft mission statement (1–2 sentences):

Step 2: Vision Development (30 minutes)
Describe your organization 3–5 years from now:
- What will we have achieved?
- How will we be different from today?
- What will others say about us?
- What specific, measurable outcomes will we have achieved?
- Draft vision statement:

Step 3: Values Identification (20 minutes)
Think of your organization at its finest:

- What principles guide our decision-making?
- What behaviors do we want to encourage?
- How do we wish to treat customers, employees, and stakeholders?
- What are we prepared to give up in order to uphold these principles?

List 3–5 core values with specific behavioral descriptions:

_____
_____
_____

Step 4: Reality Testing (15 minutes)
For each element, ask:
- Does this help us make decisions?
- Is this specific enough to guide behavior?
- Would we make different choices if this were different?
- Can we measure if we're doing this?

Strategic Analysis: Translating Intelligence into Insights

Now you will translate your environmental analysis from Chapter 5 into strategic implications. Your objective is to identify the key strategic decisions your organization should consider, based on your understanding of its environment, competition, and capabilities.

Synthesizing Your Analysis

Take your PESTEL analysis, Five Forces analysis, and SWOT analysis and look for patterns and themes:
- Convergent trends: In what direction are the environmental changes converging?
- Critical uncertainties: What unknowns would make the most significant difference to your strategy?
- Competitive dynamics: How is your competitive environment evolving?
- Capability gaps: Where do you need to build new capabilities to succeed?
- Strategic options: What different paths could you take given your situation?

Identifying Strategic Issues

Strategic issues are the underlying problems and opportunities that will determine whether you succeed or fail. They typically fall into several categories:

- Market position issues: How can you better compete in your current markets?
- Growth problems: How do you develop into new markets, products, or services?
- Capability Issues: What new capabilities must you develop or acquire?

- Efficiency concerns: How do you cut costs or enhance productivity?
- Innovation concerns: How do you keep ahead of market and technological developments?
- Stakeholder concerns: How do you better serve customers, employees, investors, and other stakeholders?

Strategic Choice Framework

For each strategic issue, you will typically have several options. Use the following format to evaluate your alternatives:

- Do nothing: Accept current trajectory and concentrate on operational excellence
- Incremental change: Make small adjustments to the current strategy
- Significant change: Alter strategy significantly while remaining in the present business
- Diversification: Develop new products/services or enter new markets
- Transformation: Fundamentally change your business model

Practical Activity: Strategic Issues and Options Analysis

Step 1: Problem Identification (20 minutes)
Based on your environmental analysis, list your top strategic issues:

Market Position Problems:
_____
_____

Growth Issues:
_____
_____

Capability Issues:
_____
_____

Step 2: Option Generation (25 minutes)
For your top 3 strategic issues, identify possible responses:

Issue 1: _____
Options:
a) _____
b) _____
c) _____

Issue 2: _____
Options:
a) _____
b) _____
c) _____

> Issue 3: _____
> Options:
> a) _____
> b) _____
> c) _____
> Step 3: Option Evaluation (15 minutes)
> For each choice, evaluate:
> - Fit with mission/vision: How well does this align with our purpose?
> - Resource requirements: What would this require in terms of money, people, and time?
> - Risk level: What might go wrong?
> - Potential impact: How much difference would this make?
> - Timeline: How long would this take to implement?

Establishing Strategic Objectives That Influence Behavior

Goals are where strategy and execution intersect. They convert your strategic decisions into concrete, quantifiable results that direct decision-making and resource allocation. Yet most companies establish goals that are either so vague as to be useless or so detailed as to be non-strategic.

To avoid falling into either of these two traps, use the SMARTER Goals Model, which is an expansion of the classic SMART model.

SMART-ER Goals Model

The SMARTER Goals model extends the classic SMART model (Specific, Measurable, Achievable, Relevant, Time-bound) by including two additional criteria:

- Exciting: Objectives ought to motivate effort and dedication
- Reviewed: Goals need to be constantly evaluated and revised

Strategic goals typically address:

- Financial performance: Revenue, profitability, cost control
- Market position: Market share, customer satisfaction, competitive position
- Operational excellence: Efficiency, productivity, quality
- Innovation and growth: New products, new markets, capability development

- Stakeholder satisfaction: Employee engagement, customer loyalty, community impact

Goal Setting Hierarchy

Create a hierarchy of objectives that relates strategic goals to operating tasks:
- Strategic objectives (3-5 year time frame): Overall outcomes that define success
- Tactical objectives (1-year horizon): Definite accomplishments that help to support strategic goals

- Operational targets (monthly/quarterly): Most essential metrics that direct daily actions

Your objectives ought to function like a system and not be in conflict with one another. Employ a balanced strategy that caters to:

- Financial results: The outcomes you need to achieve
- Customer value: How you deliver value to the people you serve
- Internal processes: The competencies you need to acquire
- Learning and development: How you build your organization's capacity

Strategic Goal Setting Worksheet

Step 1: Strategic Goal Categories (20 minutes)
  Based on your strategic analysis, establish 1–2 goals under each category:
  Financial Performance Objectives:
- Goal 1:
  _____
- Goal 2:
  _____

  Market Position Goals:
- Goal 1:
  _____
- Goal 2:
  _____

  Operational Excellence Objectives:
- Goal 1:
  _____
- Goal 2:
  _____

  Innovation/Growth Objectives:
- Goal 1:
  _____
- Goal 2:
  _____

Step 2: Goal Specification (30 minutes)
  For each goal, define:

Goal: _____

- Specific outcome: What precisely will be accomplished?
- Measurement: How will you know when you've achieved it?
- Timeline: When will this be done?
- Responsibility: Who is accountable for this goal?
- Resources: What will be required to achieve this?
- Obstacles: What could prevent achievement?
- Dependencies: What else needs to be accomplished in order for this to function?

Step 3: Goal Integration Check (10 minutes)
Discuss all objectives collectively:
- Are there any conflicting goals?
- Are the objectives mutually attainable with available resources?
- Do the goals support your mission and vision?
- Will achieving these goals represent meaningful progress?

Action Planning: Strategy to Implementation

Strategic objectives inform you of where you wish to go; action plans inform you of how you will get there. It is here that most strategic plans break down—they have lofty objectives but lack detailed maps for how to achieve them.

Effective action planning converts strategic goals into achievable projects and initiatives, delegates responsibility, allocates resources, and establishes timelines. It answers the question: "What precisely are we going to do in order to achieve our strategic goals?"

Action Planning Framework

For every strategic objective, create action plans that involve:

- Strategic initiatives: Programs or projects of a grand scale are needed to achieve the objective
- Key activities: Specific actions under each initiative
- Timelines: When the tasks will be completed
- Responsibility: Who is responsible for each activity
- Resources: What money, personnel, and additional resources are required
- Dependencies: What must happen before each activity can begin

- Success measures: How you will track progress on each project

Initiative Prioritization: You can't do everything at once. Prioritize your strategic initiatives based on:
- Impact: To what extent will this project help in realizing strategic objectives?
- Urgency: How soon is the project due?
- Resources: What will this project need in the way of money, personnel, and time?
- Dependencies: What other initiatives must succeed for this one to work?
- Risk: What are the chances of success and the expense of failure?

Resource Allocation Planning

Strategic plans fail when they demand more resources than the organization actually has. Be realistic about resource requirements and constraints:
- Financial resources: Budget requirements for each initiative
- Human resources: People needed, together with skill sets and time commitments
- Technology resources: Infrastructure, tools, and systems required
- External resources: Contractors, partners, and suppliers needed

Strategic Action Planning Template

Strategic Goal: _____

Initiative 1: _____

Objective: What exactly will this project achieve?

Key Activities:
- Activity 1: _____
    - Responsible: _____
    - Timeline: _____
    - Resources required: _____
- Activity 2: _____
    - Responsible: _____
    - Timeline: _____
    - Resources required: _____
- Activity 3: _____

- Responsible: _____
- Timeline: _____
- Resources needed: _____

Success Metrics:
- How will you monitor progress? _____
- What defines successful completion? _____

Dependencies:
- What needs to occur first? _____
- What else needs to succeed? _____

Risk Assessment:
- What could go wrong? _____
- How will you reduce these risks? _____

Resources Required:
- Budget: _____
- People: _____
- Technology: _____
- External support: _____

Implementation Systems: Making Strategy Work

Having a strategy is one thing, and following through on it is another. The most beautifully crafted plan is worthless if it doesn't actually change the way people make decisions and allocate time and resources.

Successful execution necessitates systems that:
- Share the strategy across the organization
- Align day-to-day decisions with strategic priorities
- Track progress and change course when necessary
- Hold individuals responsible for strategic outcomes

Communication and Alignment Systems

- Strategic communication plan: How will you communicate the strategy to different stakeholder groups?
    - Leadership team: Comprehensive knowledge of strategic rationale and implementation plans
    - Middle management: Clear understanding of how strategy affects their areas
    - Front-line workers: Understanding of where their work falls into strategic goals

- External stakeholders: Suitable communication regarding strategic direction
- Alignment mechanisms: How do you plan to make day-to-day decisions to reinforce strategic objectives?
  - Budget allocation: Ensure funding priorities reflect strategic priorities
  - Performance management: Map personal objectives to strategic goals
  - Decision-making processes: Integrate strategic thinking into key decisions
  - Meeting agendas: Regular discussion of strategic progress and issues

Monitoring and Control Systems

- Strategic dashboards: Critical measures that monitor movement toward strategic objectives
  - Regular review meetings: Timed assessments of strategic progress
  - Milestone tracking: Definite checkpoints for large initiatives
  - Exception reporting: Mechanisms to highlight when things are not on track
- Adaptation and Learning Systems
- Strategic plans must adapt to changing circumstances. Incorporate mechanisms for:

- Environmental monitoring: Continuous searching for changes that could affect the strategy
- Performance analysis: Continuous assessment of what works and what does not
- Strategic learning: Capturing lessons from implementation experience
- Plan revisions: Official procedures for changing strategy in response to new data

Implementation Planning Checklist

Communication Plan:
- Leadership presentation scheduled
- Management briefing materials prepared
- Employee communication plan developed.
- Stakeholder communication strategy defined

Alignment Systems:
- Budget process aligned with strategic priorities
- Performance management system updated
- Decision processes altered
- Meeting structures adjusted to include strategic focus.

Monitoring Systems:
- Strategic dashboard developed
- Review meeting schedule established.
- Milestone tracking system developed.
- Exception reporting process defined.

Resource Allocation:
- Budget requirements identified
- Staffing needs assessed
- Technology requirements determined

- External resource requirements identified

Accountability Structure:
- Strategic initiative owners assigned
- Success metrics defined
- Reporting relationships clarified
- Incentive alignment confirmed

Adaptation Mechanisms:
- Environmental monitoring system established
- Learning capture process established
- Plan update schedule set
- Change management process defined.

Leadership Development for Strategy Implementation

One area often missing from strategic plans is the leadership development necessary to execute the strategy effectively. If your strategy demands skills your current leadership group lacks, you must explicitly address this deficiency.

Strategic Leadership Evaluation

Assess your leadership team's ability to implement your strategy

- Strategic thinking: Are leaders able to think systemically about complicated problems?
- Change management: Are leaders able to lead their teams through significant changes?
- Communication: Can leaders communicate strategic priorities?
- Execution: Can leaders translate strategy into operational results?
- Collaboration: Can leaders work effectively across organizational boundaries?

Leadership Development Planning

On the basis of your evaluation, create definite plans for building leadership skills:

- Training and development: Formal programs to achieve necessary skills
- Mentoring and coaching: Key leader individual development
- Experience-based learning: Stretch assignments that build strategic skills
- External expertise: Hiring consultants or new staff members to fill capability gaps
- Succession planning: Developing next-generation leaders for critical roles

Cultural Change Management

If your strategy requires significant changes in how your organization operates, you'll need to address cultural change head-on:
- Current culture assessment: How does your current culture support or hinder strategy implementation?
- Target culture definition: Which cultural attributes do you require to execute your strategy?
- Change initiatives: Definite steps to move the culture in the intended direction
- Reinforcement mechanisms: How will you sustain cultural changes over time?
- Common Strategic Planning Mistakes and How to Avoid Them

Even well-meaning leaders can sabotage their strategic planning. The following are the most frequent errors and how to circumvent them:

The Perfection Trap

The mistake: Spending so long completing the plan that you never implement it, or planning so minutely that your plans cannot adapt.

How to avoid it: Aim for "good enough" plans that can be improved through implementation. Build in mechanisms for regular updates and adjustments.

The Participation Theater Problem

The error: Engaging in participatory planning rituals without genuinely taking input or generating commitment.

How to prevent it: Assign participants a substantive role in analysis and decision-making, rather than comment on preconceived conclusions.

The Annual Ritual Error

The mistake: Making strategic planning a once-a-year occasion rather than an ongoing process. How to avoid it: Incorporate strategic thinking into ongoing management routines. Refresh your strategy as the situation evolves, not annually.

The Implementation Afterthought

The mistake: Focusing all the energy on creating the plan and making implementation someone else's problem.

How to avoid it: Devote as much time to planning implementation as to strategic analysis. Engage the individuals who will implement the strategy in creating the action plans.

The Resource Allocation Disconnect

The error: Developing strategic plans that disregard resource realities or don't link budgets to strategic priorities.

How to avoid it: Combine strategic planning and budget planning. Be clear about resource demands and trade-offs.

The Communication Vacuum

The error: Creating a strategy in solitude and then asking yourself why individuals do not accept it.

How to avoid it: Communicate during the planning process, not just when it has finished. Help people understand not just what the strategy is, but why it makes sense.

The Measurement Mirage

The mistake: Setting up goals that sound good but cannot be actually measured, or creating measurement systems that are not connected to strategic objectives.

How to avoid it: Subject each objective to the test: "How will we know whether we're making progress?" Construct measurement systems that provide actionable feedback.

Strategic Plan Quality Evaluation

Rate your strategic plan on each dimension (1–10 scale):

Clarity and Focus:
- Mission, vision, and values provide clear direction: ___/10
- Strategic goals are specific and measurable: ___/10
- Priorities are clear and limited in number: ___/10

Environmental Alignment:
- Plan reflects thorough environmental analysis: ___/10
- Strategy addresses key external opportunities/threats: ___/10
- Plan leverages organizational strengths: ___/10

Implementation Readiness:
- Action plans are realistic and detailed: ___/10
- Resource requirements are clearly defined: ___/10
- Responsibility and accountability are allocated: ___/10

Organizational Alignment:
- Leadership team is committed to the strategy: ___/10

- Plan addresses required capability development: ___/10
- Communication plan will reach all stakeholders: ___/10

Measurement and Adaptation:
- Success metrics are defined and measurable: ___/10
- Monitoring systems will track progress: ___/10
- Mechanisms exist to adapt plan as needed: ___/10

Total Score: ___/120

Scoring Guide:
- 100–120: Strong strategic plan ready for implementation
- 80–99: Good foundation with some areas needing strengthening
- 60–79: Satisfactory but substantial improvements required
- Less than 60: Significant revision necessary prior to execution

Priority Improvement Areas:
_____
_____

Putting It All Together: Your Strategic Planning Process

Strategic planning does not need to be an annual retreat exercise. It must be an ongoing capability to navigate an uncertain and changing world. Here is a practical process to enable strategic planning as a leadership competency:

- Ongoing Strategic Thought (Monthly)
    - Environmental scanning: Occasional examination of external changes and their importance
    - Performance analysis: Evaluation of progress against strategic objectives
    - Issue identification: Identification of new opportunities and challenges
    - Strategic discussion: Collective discussion about the strategic implications of current events
- Quarterly Strategic Reviews
    - Progress monitoring: Comprehensive evaluation of strategic initiative progress
    - Plan revisions: Modifications in response to new information or changed circumstances
    - Resource reallocation: Changes in resource allocation according to strategic priorities
    - Communications updates: Stakeholder communication of strategic progress

- Annual Strategic Planning
    - Comprehensive environmental analysis: Detailed analysis of the external environment
    - Strategic position evaluation: Review of competitive position and capabilities
    - Goal setting and action planning: Setting strategic goals and action plans
    - Resource planning: Resource allocation to facilitate strategic priorities
- Strategic Plan Documentation
    - Your completed strategic plan document must be a working document, not a shelf ornament. Incorporate these elements:
        - Executive Summary (1-2 pages): Major strategic decisions and priorities
        - Situational Analysis (3-5 pages): Environmental analysis and strategic issues
        - Strategic Direction (2-3 pages): Mission, vision, values, and strategic objectives
        - Action Plans (5-10 pages): Detailed implementation plans for each of the strategic goals
        - Resource Requirements (1-2 pages): Budget and resource allocation plan

- o Implementation Systems (2-3 pages): Communication, monitoring, and accountability systems
- o Make the document brief and to the point. If it is over 20 pages, it is likely too detailed to be of use as strategic guidance.
- Make Strategy Everyone's Job

The most effective strategic plans are those in which strategic thinking becomes an integral part of how the organization operates. That is:

- o Strategic decision-making: Major decisions explicitly consider strategic implications
- o Strategic communication: Ongoing communication regarding strategic change and development
- o Strategic learning: Capturing and utilizing lessons from strategic implementation
- o Strategic development: Developing strategic thinking skills across the organization

Strategic Planning Implementation Timeline

Month 1: Foundation Setting
- Week 1: Leadership team alignment on the planning process
- Week 2: Environmental analysis and data collection
- Week 3: Stakeholder input gathering
- Week 4: Situational analysis compilation

Month 2: Strategic Development
- Week 1: Mission, vision, values review and refinement
- Week 2: Identification and analysis of strategic issues
- Week 3: Setting and prioritizing strategic goals
- Week 4: Action planning and resource allocation

Month 3: Implementation Preparation
- Week 1: Implementation system design
- Week 2: Communication plan development
- Week 3: Leadership development planning
- Week 4: Final plan review and approval

> Ongoing Implementation
> - Monthly: Strategic thinking sessions
> - Quarterly: Strategic review meetings
> - Annually: Comprehensive strategic planning cycle
>
> Key Milestones:
> - Environmental analysis done
> - Strategic goals finalized
> - Action plans developed
> - Resource allocation determined
> - Implementation systems established
> - Communication plan implemented
> - Monitoring systems functional

Wrapping It Up

Instead of creating a shining document, you write a strategic plan to build a usable map that guides your organization's actions and decisions. The best strategic plans are living documents that evolve as circumstances change, but provide consistent direction to your staff.

To succeed in strategic planning is to connect three critical pieces of the puzzle: thorough environmental analysis, clear strategic decisions, and detailed implementation planning. Ignoring any one of those elements, and your strategic plan will not deliver.

Keep in mind that strategic planning is really about making informed choices. Each component of your plan (your mission statement, your action plans) is intended to assist you and your staff in making more informed decisions about where to focus your time, energy, and resources.

Strategic planning is also a matter of building organizational capability. The act of creating a strategy collaboratively develops strategic thinking capability across your organization and aligns everyone around shared goals and priorities.

Finally, strategic planning means planning for an uncertain future. You can't say exactly what will happen, but you can position your organization to respond effectively to whatever does happen. A good strategic plan provides both direction and flexibility: clear about where you're going but adaptable in how you get there.

Key Takeaways
- Strategic planning is about making better decisions, not crafting perfect documents.

- Mission, vision, and values ought to be strategic tools to inform decision-making, not merely inspirational statements.
- Strategic goals must be specific and measurable to drive behavior and accountability.
- Implementation planning is just as crucial as strategic analysis—without excellent implementation, excellent strategies fail.
- Strategic planning should be a continuous process, not a one-time event.
- Leadership development is typically the key to strategic success—make sure your staff can execute your strategy.

Your Next Steps

- Finish the strategic planning worksheets in this chapter for your organization.
- Develop your strategic plan using the framework provided, focusing on practical implementation.
- Establish ongoing strategic planning processes rather than treating this as a one-time exercise.
- Clearly state your strategy to all of the stakeholders who need to know and support it.
- Develop strategic thinking skills in your organization.

Questions for Your Team

- What are the strategic decisions we must make from our environmental analysis?
- How do we ensure our strategic goals actually shape day-to-day decision-making? What abilities do we need to acquire to execute our strategy effectively?
- How will we measure whether our plan is succeeding, and how will we adjust if it is not?

You now have the capability to conduct your research on your environment and develop a strategic plan. However, the real challenge of leadership lies in implementation: transforming your strategic plan into tangible outcomes. In our next chapter, we will discuss how to effectively implement your strategic plan, surmounting the typical obstacles that prevent strategies from ever seeing the light of day. Strategic planning provides you with the roadmap of where you need to go. Strategic execution is what takes you there.

Chapter 7

Executing Your Strategic Plan

You've worked hard to create a strategic plan. You've conducted your environmental analysis, set clear objectives, and detailed precise action steps. Now comes the moment of truth: translating that plan into action. This is where most strategic plans die. They become beautifully crafted documents that gather dust while the organization goes about business as usual. The gap between strategy and execution is filled with the remnants of brilliant plans that never made it out of the planning room.

But here's what separates great leaders from those who just talk a good game: execution excellence. Great leaders don't just make strategies—they execute them. They put in place systems that translate strategic thinking into daily action, strategic objectives into measurable results, and strategic plans into organizational change.

The difference isn't luck or resources—it's discipline. Discipline in communication, discipline in allocating resources, discipline in measuring progress, and discipline in holding people accountable. Most of all, it's the discipline to stay focused on execution even when it's no longer trendy or as glamorous as creating the next new strategy.

> **Reflection Question**
> Consider a strategic plan you've been a part of that didn't meet its goals.
> - Was the issue with the strategy itself, or with its execution?
> - What were the specific execution gaps that made the difference?

Communicating Strategy: Making It Real for Everyone

Your strategic plan lives in your head and in a document. However, to drive results, it must be ingrained in the minds and daily behaviors of every person in your organization. Strategic communication involves building a shared understanding that informs decision-making at every level, rather than simply making presentations.

Most leaders believe they've communicated their strategy when they've presented it once at an all-hands meeting. But communication is about comprehension and commitment, not information transfer. People must understand not only what the strategy is, but also why it makes sense, how it impacts them personally, and what they need to do differently.

The Strategy Communication Framework

Level 1: Leadership Alignment
- Before implementing large-scale communication, ensure that your leadership team fully understands and is committed to the strategy. This isn't about getting people to nod in meetings—it's about creating authentic alignment around strategic decisions.
- Leadership alignment checklist:
    - Can each of the leaders explain the strategy in their own words?
    - Do they understand the logic behind key strategic decisions?
    - Are they able to link the strategy to their department's goals?
    - Are they willing to make the difficult decisions that back up the strategy?

- o Do they know how to answer questions and address concerns from their teams?

Level 2: Management Communication
- Your middle managers are the link between strategy and day-to-day operations. They must understand how strategic goals are converted into departmental objectives and individual tasks.
- Key messages for managers:
  - o How the strategy applies to their area of responsibility
  - o What specific changes are expected in their department
  - o What help and resources do they need
  - o How success will be gauged at their level
  - o What decisions are they empowered to make in support of the strategy

Level 3: Employee Engagement
- Front-line workers must be able to see how their day-to-day work is aligned with strategic success. This does not mean communicating all aspects of the strategic plan, but making it clear to people how their job makes a difference.
- Employee communication must answer:
  - o What does this imply for my work?
  - o How does my work serve these broader goals?
  - o What are my new expectations?

- What support will be provided to help me achieve these expectations?
- How will my success be evaluated?

Communication Channels and Timing

Multi-Channel Approach
- Different messages require different channels. Use a combination of:
  - In-person meetings for complicated or delicate information
  - Written communication for in-depth information, individuals must refer to
- Graphic aids to portray progress and relationships
- Interactive sessions for feedback and commitment generation

Communication Timeline
- Strategic communication is not a one-time event—it's an ongoing process:
  - Initial launch: Detailed introduction to the strategy
  - Regular updates: Progress reports and course corrections
  - Milestone celebrations: Celebrating achievements along the journey
  - Continuous reinforcement: Linking day-to-day decisions back to strategic priorities

Practical Activity: Strategy Communication Toolkit

Message Template for Leadership Team:
- Our strategic direction: _____

- Why this strategy makes sense: _____

- Critical choices that resulted in this strategy: _____

- What success looks like: _____

- Timeline and key milestones: _____

Message Template for Department Managers:
- How this strategy affects your department: _____

- Specific changes expected: _____

- Resources you'll receive: _____

- Success metrics for your area: _____

- Decision-making power you possess: _____

> Message Template for Front-line Employees:
> - What this means for your day-to-day work:
>   _____
>
> - How your job helps achieve success:
>   _____
>
> - New expectations or responsibilities:
>   _____
>
> - Training and support you will receive:
>   _____
>
> - How you will measure your performance:
>   _____

Setting Clear Objectives and Milestones

Strategic objectives are worthless unless they're converted into specific, measurable targets that inform daily decision-making. However, here's where most leaders go wrong: they either set objectives that are so vague they can't be acted upon or so detailed that they micromanage execution. Strong strategic objectives establish a clear roadmap from where you are today to where you need to be, with significant milestones that enable you to measure progress and course-correct along the way.

The Cascade Model

Strategic objectives should cascade throughout your organization in progressively specific terms:
- Strategic Level (3-5 years): Broad outcomes that define success
    - Example: "Be the premier sustainable packaging solutions provider in our region"
- Tactical Level (1 year): Definite achievements supporting strategic goals
    - Example: "Create three new eco-friendly product lines and gain 15% market share in the sustainable packaging sector."
- Operational Level (Monthly/Quarterly): Measurable tasks leading to tactical achievement
    - Example: "Finish product development for biodegradable food containers by Q2 and have two major retail partnerships by Q3"

Milestone Planning

Milestones are your early warning system. They inform you if you are on target before it is too late to make a change. Good milestones are:
- Meaningful: They reflect real progress toward strategic goals

- Measurable: You can objectively determine whether they've been achieved
- Time-bound: They possess clear deadlines
- Actionable: Missing a milestone triggers specific responses

Milestone Framework:
- 30-60-90 Day Quick Wins: Initial accomplishments that gain momentum
- Quarterly Checkpoints: Regular assessment of progress versus annual goals
- Annual Reviews: Overall assessment of strategic development
- Strategic Milestones: Important achievements that signify significant progress toward long-term objectives

Resource Allocation: Spending Your Money Where Your Strategy Is

Nothing more clearly indicates an organization's real priorities than its resource allocation. You can have the most visionary strategic plan in the world, but if your budget, people, and focus are elsewhere, your strategy will fail.

Reasonable resource allocation involves making tough choices about what to invest in and what to cut, which jobs to prioritize, and which projects to postpone. It means coordinating your resource choices with your strategic choices, even when that makes you uncomfortable.

Financial Resource Allocation

- Strategic Initiatives: Direct investments in strategic priorities
- Core Operations: Resources needed to maintain current performance
- Innovation and Development: Investments in future capabilities
- Contingency: Resources held in reserve for unexpected opportunities or challenges

Resource Allocation Calculator

Strategic Priority Assessment:

Priority 1: _____
Budget Needed: $_____
Anticipated ROI: _____

Priority 2: _____
Budget Needed: $_____
Anticipated ROI: _____

Priority 3: _____
Budget Needed: $_____
Anticipated ROI: _____

Current Resource Allocation:
- Strategic initiatives: ____% of budget
- Core operations: ____% of budget
- Development/innovation: ____% of budget
- Contingency: ____% of budget

Gap Analysis:
- Strategic funding gap: $_____
- Reallocation opportunities: _____
- Additional funds required: $_____

Human Resource Allocation

Your personnel are your most vital strategic asset. Strategic implementation demands not only the correct number of individuals, but the right individuals in the right positions at the right time.

Strategic Staffing Framework

- Core team members: Individuals who are full-time for strategic initiatives
- Project contributors: People who contribute specific expertise part-time
- Strategic supporters: Individuals who offer infrastructure and support
- Change champions: People who help drive behavioral and cultural changes

Skills and Capacity Planning

- What new skills do we have to acquire or develop?
- Which current team members have the skills needed for strategic roles?
- Where do we have capacity constraints that could limit implementation?
- What investments in training and development are needed?

Implementation through Action Plans and Project Management

Strategic plans are realized through projects and initiatives. This is where the rubber hits the road—where strategic thinking is translated into concrete actions with timelines, budgets, and responsible owners. Effective project implementation means that strategic initiatives must be treated as the significant projects they are, with the appropriate project management rigor and governance mechanisms in place.

Project Management Framework for Strategic Implementation

Project Charter for Strategic Initiatives
- Project Purpose: Why this project is vital to strategic goals
- Success Criteria: Clear, measurable outcomes that define success
- Timeline: Key events and ultimate completion date
- Resources: Budget, personnel, and other resources needed
- Risks: Possible challenges and mitigation measures
- Dependencies: What else needs to happen for this project to succeed

Project Governance Structure
- Strategic Sponsor: Senior leader responsible for strategic success
- Project Owner: Person responsible for day-to-day project management
- Core Team: Individuals committed to project implementation
- Steering Committee: The group that provides direction and removes obstacles

Strategic Project Dashboard

Track the health of your strategic implementation with a simple dashboard that shows:

Strategic Initiative: _____

Overall Status:
- Green
- Yellow
- Red

Progress Measures:
- Timeline: ___% complete, _____ days ahead/behind schedule
- Budget: ___% spent, $_____ over/under budget
- Milestones: _____ out of _____ completed on schedule
- Quality: Above/meeting/below expectations

Key Accomplishments This Period:
1. _____
2. _____
3. _____

Major Issues/Risks:
1. _____

```
2._____
3._____
Next Period Priorities:
1._____
2._____
3._____
```

Monitoring Progress with KPIs and Periodic Reviews

You can't manage what you don't measure. Strategic execution requires systematic measurement of progress against goals, with periodic reviews that permit course adjustments before problems become crises.

However, this also meant that measurement systems must drive behavior, not just report it. The metrics you choose will determine what people prioritize and how they spend their time.

Strategic KPI Framework

- Financial Metrics: Revenue, profitability, cost management

- Customer Measures: Satisfaction, retention, market share

- Operational Metrics: Productivity, efficiency, quality

- Innovation Metrics: New products, process improvements, capability development
- People Metrics: Engagement, retention, capability development

Review Rhythm

- Weekly Operational Reviews:
    - Immediate execution issues focus
        - What's on schedule and what's lagging?
        - What obstacles need to be removed?
        - What support do teams need?
- Monthly Strategic Reviews:
    - Concentrate on advancements made toward strategic goals
        - Are we meeting our milestones?
        - What are the trends in our metrics?
        - What do we need to change?
- Quarterly Strategic Reviews:
    - Focus on strategic direction and resource allocation
        - Do our strategic assumptions remain valid?
        - Do we need to modify our goals or timelines?
        - What are we learning from our execution?

Building a Culture of Accountability

Accountability is what converts good intentions into actual results. It focuses on creating a culture where people take responsibility for their results and follow through on commitments, rather than relying on blame or punishment.

Genuine accountability has four components: clear expectations, adequate resources, regular check-ins, and consequences, both positive and negative, for performance.

The Accountability Framework: Clear Ownership

Every strategic objective and project requires one person who is ultimately accountable for results. That person doesn't have to do it all, but they own the result.

- Defined Success: Accountability requires specific, measurable definitions of success. Vague goals create wiggle room that destroys accountability.

- Regular Check-ins: Accountability isn't an annual performance review—it's a regular conversation about progress, obstacles, and support needs.

- Consequences: Both positive rewards for success and constructive responses to failure. Without consequences, accountability is meaningless.

Practical Activity: Accountability Planning

Strategic Objective: _____
Accountable Person: _____

Success Metrics:
    1. _____
    _____

    2. _____
    _____

    3. _____
    _____

Check-in Time:
- Weekly status reports:
  _____

- Monthly progress checks:
  _____

- Quarterly assessments:
  _____

Support Provided:
- Resources:
  _____

- Training:
  _____

- Authority:
  _____

Recognition for Success:
- Individual recognition: _____

- Team recognition: _____

- Organizational recognition: _____

Response to Performance Issues:
- Early warning triggers: _____

- Support escalation: _____

- Process for improving performance: _____

Being Adaptable to Change and Continuously Improving

No strategic plan survives contact with reality unscathed. The business environment shifts, new opportunities arise, unexpected challenges emerge, and you learn things during the execution process that were not obvious while planning.

The best strategic leaders build adaptability into their execution process. They monitor progress against the plan, and also environmental shifts that would require revisions to the plan.

Change Adaptation Framework
- Environmental Monitoring: Regular scanning of developments that are likely to affect your strategy
- Performance Analysis: Ongoing evaluation of what is working and what is not
- Learning Capture: Systematic collection of lessons learned from execution
- Plan Evolution: Formal processes for changing strategy based on new information
- Continuous Improvement Process:
    - Monthly Learning Reviews:
        - What's going better than anticipated?
        - What's not working as planned?
        - What did we learn about our market, customers, or capabilities?
        - What adjustments should we consider?
    - Quarterly Strategy Updates:
        - What changes in our environment affect our strategic assumptions?
        - How should we modify our objectives or timelines?

- What reallocations of resources are necessary?
- How do we communicate changes to the organization?

Change Adaptation Checklist:

Environmental Changes:
- Market conditions: Any significant changes?
- Competitive Environment: New Threats or Opportunities?
- Technology: Developments that Impact Our Strategy?
- Regulations: Alterations that Affect Our Plans?
- Economic conditions: Changes that influence resources or demand?

Execution Learning:
- Performance: Are We Meeting Our Milestones?
- Resource Usage: Are We on Budget and Schedule?
- Capability Development: Are We Building the Necessary Skills?
- Stakeholder feedback: What are our employees and customers telling us?

Strategic Changes Required:

> - Objective modifications: Do goals need to be revised?
> - Resource Allocation: Should the Funding Be Redirected?
> - Timeline adjustments: Do deadlines require revision?
> - Approach changes: Should we modify our methods?
>
> Communication Requirements:
> - Leadership team: What do they need to know?
> - Management team: How are changes impacting their areas?
> - Employees: What should they understand about modifications?
> - Stakeholders: Who else needs to be informed?

Making Execution Everyone's Responsibility

Strategic execution is not just the job of senior management or project managers. It's *everyone's* job. The best strategic executions are those where every person in the organization understands how their daily tasks contribute to the organization's strategic accomplishment.

This goes beyond communication to infusing strategic thinking into day-to-day operations, decision processes, and performance management systems.

Integration Strategies

- Decision-Making Integration: Train people to ask "How does this support our strategic objectives?" before making significant decisions.

- Meeting Integration: Make strategic progress a standing agenda item in team meetings.

- Performance Integration: Link individual performance objectives to strategic goals.

- Communication Integration: Celebrate victories and share stories that link everyday work to strategic success on a regular basis.

Wrapping It Up

Strategic execution is where leadership credibility is won or lost. Anyone can create an impressive strategic plan, but only disciplined leaders can turn that plan into results.

What distinguishes successful from unsuccessful strategic initiatives is back to basics: clear communication, disciplined resource allocation, methodical monitoring, genuine accountability, and the flexibility to change course as you learn.

Keep in mind that execution is not a phase that follows planning—it needs to be incorporated into your plan from the very beginning. The most effective strategic plans are those that are created with execution in mind, including definite accountability, quantifiable milestones, and realistic resource demands.

Most importantly, strategic execution is a leadership capability, not a one-time project. The leaders who consistently deliver strategic results are those who build execution discipline into their daily operations.

Key Takeaways

- Strategic execution is where good plans become great results

- Communication should generate understanding and commitment, not merely information conveyance
- Resource allocation decisions reflect your real strategic priorities
- Regular monitoring with periodic reviews allows for course corrections
- Accountability needs to have clear ownership, defined success, and significant consequences
- Flexibility and ongoing improvement are key to long-term prosperity

Your Next Steps

- Formulate your strategy communication plan based on the templates given
- Develop resource allocation plans that map budget and personnel to strategic priorities
- Establish monitoring systems with meaningful KPIs and regular review cycles
- Establish accountability mechanisms with well-defined ownership and penalties
- Apply change adaptation processes to ensure strategic relevance

Questions for Your Team

- How effectively are we communicating our strategy throughout the organization?
- Where are the discrepancies between our declared strategic priorities and the way we actually allocate resources?
- What accountability systems do we need to strengthen to enable implementation?
- How quickly do we detect and respond to changes that affect our strategy?

Strategic planning provides the map. Strategic execution takes you to the destination. In our next segment, we'll learn how to master the communication skills that enable both strategy and execution through people.

PART III: COMMUNICATE

How You Connect with People

Chapter 8

Mastering Leadership Communication

Here's a question that might embarrass you: How often have you walked away from a conversation thinking you were clear, only to discover later the other person took away something completely different from what you intended?

If you're like most executives, this happens more often than you'd care to admit. You think you're being clear, concise, and compelling, but somehow your message gets lost in translation. Your team is confused about priorities, stakeholders misread your position, and even simple instructions somehow get tangled up.

You can say all the right things, but if people don't understand them the way you meant, your leadership suffers. And the difference between those two things is where leadership success is usually made or broken.

Most leaders focus on improving their speaking, yet communication encompasses far more than just speaking. It's reading your audience, selecting the appropriate medium, controlling your nonverbal cues, and achieving real understanding. It engages people in a way that motivates action, fosters trust, and yields results.

This chapter will equip you with the real-world skills to be a more effective communicator—not just one who communicates well, but one who genuinely connects with others and influences outcomes through the practice of strategic communication.

Reflection Question

Think about the most effective communicator you know personally.
- What specifically do they do that makes their communication so effective?
- Is it what they say, how they say it, or something else entirely?

Understanding Communication: It's More Than Words

Most individuals, when they consider communication, consider words. However, studies indicate that words only contribute to approximately 7% of the effect of face-to-face communication. The remaining 93% is a result of how you say it (tone, pace, volume) and your body language (posture, gestures, eye contact).

This is because, as a leader, you are constantly communicating even when you are silent. The look on your face during a team meeting, your stance when someone comes to you with a problem, your tone of voice when you respond to emails—all of these convey messages that are frequently stronger than your words.

The Three Dimensions of Leadership Communication

Verbal Communication: Your Word Choice

Your words convey the content of your message, but they also express your thoughts, values, and priorities.

- Effective leaders choose words that are
    - Precise: Stating exactly what you mean with no uncertainty
    - Appropriate: Matching your language to your audience and situation

- Compelling: Employing words that inspire and encourage action
- Respectful: Treating other people with dignity, even in difficult conversations

Paraverbal Communication: How You Say It

This includes your tone, pace, loudness, and pitch. These elements can completely change the meaning of your words. Consider how differently "Great job" is received when said with enthusiasm versus sarcasm.

- Important paraverbal features of leaders
    - Tone: Reveals your attitude and emotional state
    - Pace: Confidently displays and aids understanding
    - Volume: Indicates authority and consideration,
    - Inflection: Gives emphasis and holds attention

Nonverbal Communication: What Your Body Says

Body language often conveys your true sentiments and attitudes, occasionally in conflict with your verbal communication. Being a leader, your nonverbal cues establish the tone for all interactions.

- Key nonverbal elements
    - Posture: Displays confidence, openness, and interest

- Eye contact: Establishes trust and conveys respect
- Facial expressions: Show your genuine reactions
- Gestures: Accentuate points and express enthusiasm
- Proximity: Shows comfort and authority

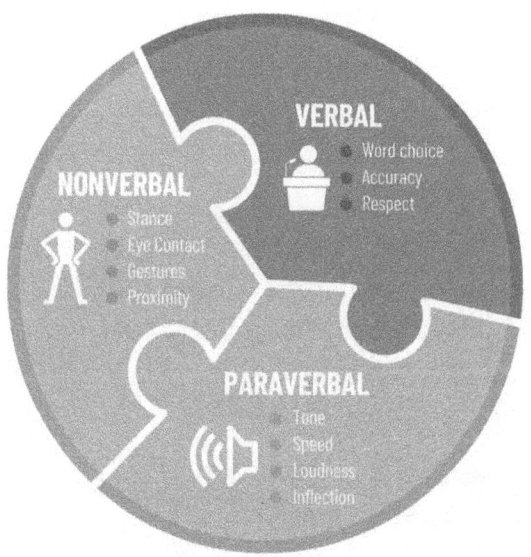

Communication Congruence

The most effective communication occurs when your verbal, paraverbal, and nonverbal messages are all congruent. If they aren't, people will naturally trust the nonverbal cues over the words.

For instance, if you say "I'm looking forward to this project" and you're not making eye contact, talking in a monotone, and folding your arms, people will trust your body language more than your words.

Practical Activity: Communication Style Questionnaire

Step 1: Self-Assessment (20 minutes)
Rate yourself on each communication dimension (1-10 scale)
- Verbal Skills:
    - Clarity of expression: ___/10
    - Vocabulary appropriateness: ___/10
    - Persuasive language use: ___/10
    - Active listening: ___/10
- Paraverbal Skills:
    - Tone management: ___/10
    - Speaking pace: ___/10
    - Volume control: ___/10
    - Vocal variety: ___/10
- Nonverbal Skills:
    - Confident posture: ___/10
    - Appropriate eye contact: ___/10

> - Facial expressiveness: ___/10
> - Meaningful gestures: ___/10
>
> **Step 2: Feedback Collection (Next 2 weeks)**
> - Ask three trusted colleagues
>   - "What are my communication strengths?"
>   - "Where can I enhance my communication effectiveness?"
>   - "When have you seen me communicate most/least effectively?"
>
> **Step 3: Gap Analysis (15 minutes)**
> - What is the most considerable discrepancy between your self-assessment and other people's feedback?
> - Which dimension of communication requires the most improvement?
> - What specific situations challenge your communication effectiveness most?

Communication Factors: Method, Mass, and Audience

Being a good communicator is not just about your message—it's also about choosing the proper method, understanding your audience size, and being attentive to your specific listeners. Getting any one of those wrong can compromise even the best content.

Method: Choosing the Right Communication Channel

Different messages require different delivery methods. The reception of your message and what people do next are determined by the channel you utilize.

- Face-to-Face Communication
    - Best for: Sensitive or complicated issues, building relationships, subtle conversations
    - Advantages: Full range of communication, immediate feedback, personal touch
    - Difficulty: Time-consuming, difficult with large groups, no record kept
- Video Calls/Conferencing
    - Best for: Virtual team meetings, presentations, maintaining personal touch at a distance
    - Advantages: Visual cues, inexpensive for distance, can be taped
    - Challenges: Technical issues, "Zoom fatigue," and reduced informal interaction
- Phone/Audio Calls

- o Best for: Quick decisions, confidential matters, building personal rapport
- o Advantages: Instant response, personal touch, no visual distractions
- o Challenges: No visual cues, multitasking is easier, and it is more difficult to read reactions
- Email
  - o Best for: In-depth information, documentation, formal communication
  - o Advantages: Permanent record, time to consider, effective for multiple recipients
  - o Challenges: Lacks tone of voice, can be easily misinterpreted, and too much use causes inbox overload
- Written Communications (Memos, Reports)
  - o Best for: Policy announcements, complex information, reference information
  - o Advantages: In-depth content, lasting record, standard message
  - o Challenges: One-way communication, no immediate feedback, can be impersonal
- Social/Digital Platforms
  - o Best for: General announcements, informal updates, community building
  - o Advantages: Extensive reach, interactive, creates transparency
  - o Disadvantages: Public in nature, less control, requires frequent management

Mass: Adjusting to Audience Size

- The size of your audience automatically changes how you should talk. What works for one person may not be enough for a hundred, and the reverse is also true.
    - One-on-One Communication
        - Focus on personal connection and individual needs
        - Use conversational tone and interactive dialogue
        - Adjust your style according to instant feedback
        - Address specific concerns and motives
    - Small Groups (2-10 persons)
        - Invite participation from all
        - Use cooperative problem-solving and dialogue
        - Keep eye contact with all parties
        - Facilitate instead of merely presenting
    - Medium Groups (10-50 individuals)
        - Balance presentation and interaction
        - Utilize visual aids and formal agendas
        - Encourage questions, but control discussion time
        - Ensure remote participants are engaged

- Large Groups (50+ individuals)
    - Focus on a clear, engaging presentation
    - Use storytelling and visual elements
    - Restrict interaction to question-and-answer sessions
    - Consider multiple communication methods

Audience: Knowing Your Listeners

Every audience is different, and effective communicators adjust their style based on whom they are addressing.

Audience Analysis Framework:
- Professional Background
    - What's their expertise level in your topic?
    - What professional pressures are they facing?
    - Which language and examples will bridge?
- Relationship to You
    - What's the power dynamic?
    - What is the history of your relationship?
    - What is the proper degree of formality?
- Motivations and Interests
    - What matters most to them?
    - What problems would they like to solve?
    - What's in it for them?

- Communication Preferences
    - Do they like details or the big picture?
    - Are they analytical or action-oriented?
    - What communication style do they respond to best?

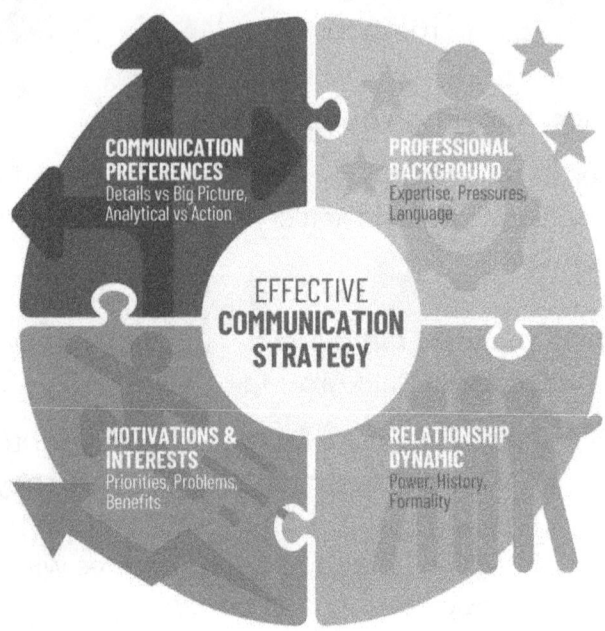

Overcoming Communication Barriers

Despite an ideal technique, communication may fail because of barriers that get in the way of your message being received and interpreted as planned. Effective leaders anticipate these barriers and devise strategies to overcome them.

Language Barriers

Language differences go beyond speaking different native languages. They include jargon, technical terms, cultural references, and various levels of language sophistication.

- Types of Language Barriers
    - Technical jargon: Utilizing technical words that others fail to comprehend
    - Cultural references: Idioms, phrases, or examples that do not translate across cultures
    - Educational differences: Assuming knowledge or terminology that others may not have
    - Generation gaps: Communication styles or references that do not connect with different age groups
- Strategies to Overcome Language Barriers:
    - Recognize and Identify
        - Identify when there are language differences
        - Ask clarifying questions to ensure understanding
        - Pay attention to confused expressions or a lack of engagement
    - Simplify Without Condescending

- Write in plain, straightforward language without patronizing individuals
 - Replace jargon with plain English descriptions
 - Provide context for unfamiliar terms or concepts
- Use Visual Support
 - Use diagrams, charts, or pictures to aid verbal communication
 - Use examples and analogies that everyone can identify with
 - Give written summaries of main points
- Involve Translators or Cultural Liaisons
 - For important communication, use professional interpreters
 - Identify bilingual team members who can help bridge language gaps
 - Invest in translation services for key documents

Cultural Barriers

Cultural differences influence language, but they also impact communication styles, decision-making processes, and relationship expectations.

- Common Cultural Communication Differences
  - Direct versus indirect communication: Some cultures appreciate

straightforwardness, others appreciate tact
    - Hierarchy awareness: Different expectations for formal vs. informal communication
    - Time orientation: Different attitudes towards punctuality, deadlines, and meeting structure
    - Nonverbal norms: Variations in the meaning of eye contact, personal space, and gestures
- Cultural Adaptation Strategies
    - Investigate cultural communication norms prior to significant interactions
    - Politely ask cultural questions when you're unsure
    - Observe and adjust to other people's communication styles
    - Build relationships before talking business in relationship-oriented cultures

Geographic and Time Barriers

Physical distance and time zone differences present unique challenges for effective leadership communication.
- Distance Communication Challenges:
    - Decreased nonverbal cues in virtual communication

- Technical problems disrupting message understandability
- Harder to form personal relationships
- Informal communication opportunities are lost
* Time Zone Management:
    - Alternate meeting times to spread the inconvenience evenly
    - Use asynchronous communication for non-urgent matters
    - Be explicit about response time expectations
    - Consider cultural holidays and work schedules

Paraverbal Skills: The Power of How You Say It

Your paraverbal communication—your voice usage—can make all the difference between confidence and perplexity, motivation and apprehension. They are skills that are often assumed, yet they are critical to effective leadership.

Mastering Your Tone

Tone mirrors your attitude, emotional state, and relationship with your audience. The exact words may encourage or discourage, based solely on your tone.
* Tone Elements to Control
    - Warmth: Shows concern and builds rapport

- Confidence: Exhibits authority and competency
- Enthusiasm: Creates energy and motivation
- Respect: Upholds dignity in every interaction
- Tone Adaptation to Various Situations
    - Coaching dialogue: Warm and supportive
    - Strategic presentations: Confident and compelling
    - Crisis communication: Calm and authoritative
    - Celebration moments: Enthusiastic and appreciative
- Controlling Your Speed
    - Speech rate influences understanding and impression. Too quick, and individuals cannot keep up; too slow, and they lose interest or doubt your confidence.

Volume and Projection

Volume is not merely a matter of being loud enough to be heard—it is a matter of showing confidence, respect for your audience, and setting the appropriate mood.

Volume Considerations:

- Room size and acoustics: Compensate for the physical space
- Audience size: The bigger groups usually require more volume
- Emotional tone: Balance volume with the emotional content of the message

Cultural norms:
- Certain cultures favor quieter communication
- Utilizing Inflection and Emphasis: The upward and downward movement of your voice gives meaning to your words and prevents listeners from tuning out.
- Monotone speaking is public enemy number one of good communication.

Inflection Techniques:
- Rise for questions: Allow your voice to rise when you ask questions
- Fall for statements: Declarative sentences end with downward inflection
- Stress key words: Utilize changes in volume and pitch to stress significant points
- Create rhythm: Vary your inflection to maintain interest

Daily Communication Practice Plan

- Week 1-2: Developing Tone
    - Daily practice: Tape yourself while you're on the phone, then listen back for tone
    - Exercise: Practice repeating "Thank you for bringing this to my attention" using various tones (appreciative, annoyed, curious, concerned)
    - Application: In every conversation, make a deliberate choice of tone prior to speaking
- Week 3-4: Pace Control
    - Daily practice: Read news stories aloud at varying speeds, timing yourself
    - Exercise: Try to explain a difficult idea both rapidly and slowly, observing differences in comprehension
    - Application: Vary your tempo in presentations, slowing down for important points
- Week 5-6: Volume and Projection
    - Daily practice: Practice delivering speeches to imaginary groups of different sizes
    - Exercise: Record yourself talking in different rooms, adjusting volume as necessary

> - o Application: Purposely vary your volume according to room size and audience requirements

Nonverbal Communication Mastery

Your body language speaks before you do and continues to talk after you've stopped. As a leader, nonverbal communication is even more critical since people take cues from you regarding confidence, sincerity, and emotional state.

Posture: Your Foundation of Authority

Your stance constitutes the foundation of your nonverbal presence. It affects both how others perceive you and how you perceive yourself.

Confident Leadership Stance:

- Upright spine: Shows energy and interest
- Relaxed shoulders: Demonstrates comfort and control
- Balanced position: Conveys stability and grounding
- Open positioning: Implies accessibility and honesty

Eye Contact: Establishing Connection and Trust. Eye contact is one of your most powerful nonverbal tools. It fosters trust, shows respect, demonstrates confidence, and allows you to gauge reactions.

- Eye Contact Guidelines:
    - Duration: 3-5 seconds at a time, then look away briefly
    - Distribution: Establish eye contact with everyone in a group, not just dominant speakers
    - Cultural sensitivity: Adjust to the cultural norms of eye contact
    - Authenticity: Natural eye contact, not staring or avoiding
- Successful Leadership Gestures:
    - Open palm gestures: Indicate honesty and openness
    - Descriptive gestures: Assist in describing size, shape, or direction
    - Emphatic gestures: Highlight crucial points
    - Inclusive gestures: Engage people in the conversation
- Gesture Guidelines:
    - Size: Match gesture size to audience size—bigger gestures for larger groups
    - Frequency: Utilize gestures naturally, not continually or never
    - Cultural awareness: Be aware that gesture meanings vary across cultures

- o Authenticity: Utilize gestures that are spontaneous to your character

Speaking Like a STAR: Structuring Your Communication for Impact

A highly effective technique for concise, persuasive communication is the STAR method: Situation, Task, Action, Result. It enables you to organize your thoughts, create memorable stories, and make your communication more engaging and actionable.

The STAR Communication Method Explained

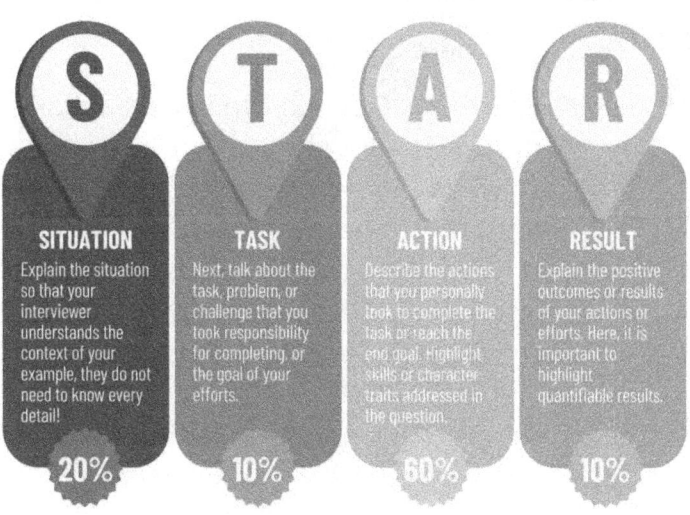

- Situation: Establish the context by concisely explaining the situation
- Task: Explain what needed to be done or what issue needed to be resolved
- Action: Describe specifically the actions taken to correct the situation
- Result: Share the results and lessons learned

This model is effective for everything ranging from responding to interview questions to providing project status reports to sharing success stories that inspire your team.

STAR in Different Communication Contexts

- Project Updates:
    - Situation: "Our customer satisfaction ratings fell 15% last quarter."
    - Task: "We needed to get to root causes and make improvements fast."
    - Action: "We conducted customer interviews, analyzed complaint data, and redesigned our response process."
    - Outcome: "Recovery of satisfaction scores to former levels within 6 weeks, and we now have improved early warning systems."
- Team Motivation:
    - Situation: "Last year, we encountered our toughest competitive challenge yet."
    - Task: "We had to rethink our go-to-market strategy completely."
    - Action: "The group worked together to explore new approaches, try out new solutions, and implement changes rapidly."
    - Result: "We not only defended our market position but also achieved 12%

market share and built capabilities that serve us today."
- Problem-Solving Discussions:
    - Scenario: "We're having quality issues with our new product line."
    - Task: "We need to identify the root cause and implement fixes without delaying the launch."
    - Action: "Here's what I recommend we do." (enumerate specific actions): "This should solve the quality issues while still keeping us on schedule for launch."

Making STAR Stories Compelling

- Use Specific Details: Generalizations that lack specificity do not capture people's interest. Utilize specific figures, timeframes, and examples.

- Focus on Learning: Even when writing about failures, emphasize what was learned and how future performance was improved.

- Include Others: Share credit and highlight team contributions to build relationships and credibility.

- Match the Message to the Audience: Select examples and details that are relevant to your target audience.

Complex Conversation Scripts Using STAR Framework

Script 1: Performance Issue
 "I wanted to talk about what's going on with the Johnson project (Situation). We promised to deliver the first phase by the 15th (Task). The deliverables were late by three days and lacked some essential elements (Action/Current State). This jeopardizes the whole project schedule and damages our credibility with the client (Result/Impact). Why don't we talk about what occurred and how we can avoid this in the future?"

Script 2: Strategic Disagreement
 "I know you have reservations about the new market strategy (Situation). Your role is to ensure we make informed investment choices (Task). You've raised some valid points regarding resource allocation and market timing (Action/Their Perspective). I believe we can alleviate these concerns while still taking a strategic step forward (Result/Desired Outcome). Let me provide further data which may change your viewpoint."

Script 3: Team Conflict Resolution
 "I've noticed some tension between the marketing and sales teams around the quality of leads (Situation). Both teams need to work well

> together if we are to achieve our revenue targets (Task). The tension present is affecting both morale within the teams and our customer service (Action/Current Impact). I'd like to discuss it to resolve these issues and establish better working relationships going forward (Result/Desired Outcome)."

Building Your Communication Feedback System

Ongoing improvement in communication takes systematic feedback and practice. Here is how you can create your own development system.

Establishing Your Communication Feedback Loop

- Regular Feedback Sources:
    - Peer observers: Your peers who come to your presentations and meetings
    - Team members: Direct reports who experience your communication daily
    - Mentors or coaches: Effective leaders who can provide objective guidance
    - Professional feedback: Training or formal communication evaluation
- Feedback Gathering Methods:
    - Post-meeting surveys: Quick feedback on single communication events

- Regular one-on-ones: Continuing dialogue on communication effectiveness
- 360-degree reviews: Feedback from every angle
- Video analysis: Recording and analyzing your own communication

- Communication Practice Opportunities
  - Low-Stakes Practice:
    - Internal presentations: Practice new skills on familiar audiences
    - One-on-one discussions: Try out varied strategies within secure environments
    - Team meetings: Experiment with new discussion or facilitation techniques
    - Email communication: Establish tone and clarity of written communication
  - High-Stakes Application:
    - Board presentations: Utilize the finest communication abilities in high-stakes situations
    - Crisis communication: Use techniques when the stakes are highest
    - Public speaking: Seize the chance to address external audiences

- o Media interviews: Rehearse clear, concise communication under stress

Wrapping It Up

Leadership communication mastery involves far more than just talking a good game. It's about fostering genuine understanding, building trust, motivating action, and engaging people on a level that yields results.

The most effective leaders are those who acknowledge that communication is a strategic competence that needs ongoing improvement. They realize that each interaction is an opportunity to form meaningful relationships, drive results, and shape the future they desire.

Keep in mind that communication skills are not only about your technique—it's about being genuine. The most compelling communication occurs when your words, your paraverbal cues, and your nonverbal presence are all congruent with your authentic intentions and values.

Key Takeaways

- Communication is what other people hear, not necessarily what you speak

- Verbal, paraverbal, and nonverbal components need to be congruent for optimum effect
- Different audiences, contexts, and purposes require different approaches to communication
- Communication barriers can be bridged with consciousness and specific measures
- The STAR framework provides structure for clear, compelling communication
- Regular feedback and practice are crucial to improve communication

Your Next Steps

- Fill in the communication style questionnaire and identify your development needs.
- Use the daily communication practice plan to build specific skills
- Create your own feedback system for ongoing communication improvement
- Apply the STAR technique in various communication scenarios
- Develop scripts and strategies for your most difficult communication dilemmas

Questions for Your Team

- What are the best communication strategies to fit our team culture and dynamics?

- Where do we notice the most significant communication gaps within our organization?
- How can we create more effective feedback loops to enhance communication?
- Which communication barriers must we overcome to work more effectively together?

Communication is the bridge between your leadership vision and your followers' reality. Master this bridge, and you can lead people anywhere. In our next chapter, we'll learn to apply your communication skills actually to understand and engage your followers.

Chapter 9

Understanding and Engaging Your Followers

You've formed your character, demonstrated your ability, exhibited the right behaviors, and developed a solid strategic plan. You communicate effectively and execute with intention. But what sets decent leaders apart from truly transformational leaders is the depth at which they understand and relate to the people they are leading.

Most leaders assume they understand their people because they observe their performance, attend their meetings, and review their projects. But knowing followers is far more profound than knowing their work performance. It is understanding their motivations, their dreams, their problems, and what makes the very best work come out of them.

When you understand your followers, everything else falls into place. Communication works better because you know the type of information processing each individual has. Motivation works better because you understand what motivates each individual. Problem-solving works better because you've earned the trust it takes for open conversation.

In this chapter, you will learn how to systemically understand and mobilize your followers to build relationships, improve performance, and establish the basis of sustained leadership performance.

Reflection Question

Consider your all-time best boss.

- What did that person know about you that assisted so significantly with what you did and were pleased doing at work?
- What did that person do that was reflective of that awareness?

Strategic Significance of Followership Knowledge

Knowing your followers is essential for being a successful leader. When you understand what works for each individual within the team, you can place them in positions that utilize their strengths, provide them with feedback where they can receive it, and encourage their best work.

Suppose we have:
- Scenario A: You have a team player who consistently misses deadlines. You correct this by imposing tighter deadlines and adding supervision. This continues, and frustration builds up on both sides.
- Scenario B: You have the same team member missing deadlines. But through understanding conversations, you discover they're overwhelmed by the volume of requests and don't know how to prioritize. You work together to create a priority system and establish boundaries. Performance improves dramatically.

The change is in your mindset of comprehending the person within the performance.

Why Leaders Fail to Appreciate Followers

- Time Pressure: Managers are often too busy to engage in in-depth discussions about individual employees' needs and motivations.
- Assumption-Making: We assume that we know others based on limited interactions or superficial knowledge.

- One-Size-Fits-All Thinking: It is easier to handle all individuals the same way instead of tailoring your approach to individual differences.

- Fear of Getting Too Personal: Some leaders are concerned that knowing their followers too intimately blurs professional boundaries.

- Inability to Communicate Effectively: Scant few leaders ever learned how to communicate at a nontransactional level or to ask relevant questions.

Composing Your Questioning Toolkit

To truly understand your followers, you must listen carefully and frame your questions effectively. Here are some examples of how leaders generate operational questions:

"Is the project on schedule?"
"When is this going to occur?"
"Are there issues about which I should sit up and take notice?"

Understanding questions are more profound. They exceed motivational levels, addressing issues and setting goals that elicit the best effort from people.

Open questions: Fostering Space for Discovery

Open-ended questions elicit significant responses and give those questioned permission to reveal what is truly on their minds. They are initiated with phrases such as "what," "how," "why," "when," "where," and "who."

- Examples of Understanding-Focused Open Questions:
    - "What de-energizes you and what re-energizes you?"
    - "How do you react when you receive criticism?"
    - "What can we do to make you feel more supported?"
    - "When do you do your finest thinking and problem-solving?"
    - "What are your career development goals?"

Closed Questions: Completion of Certain Information

Whereas open-ended questions unlock space, closed questions uncover particular preferences, circumstances, or requirements. They are mostly yes/no or factual data questions.

- Examples of Good Closed Questions:
    - "Do you like instructions in writing or oral?"
    - "Are you more productive at specific points of the day?"

- "Would you prefer greater freedom of choice of projects?"
- "Is the work at its usual volume?"

Probing Questions: Exploring Further

Probing questions enable you to understand the reasoning, feelings, and context behind other individuals' answers. They are revealing of interest and uncover points of information that can foster deepened work relationships.

- Types of Probing Questions:
    - Clarification Questions:
        - "What do you mean when you say you need greater support?"
    - Example Questions:
        - "Tell me about a time when you were most concentrated at work."
    - Feel Questions:
        - "How did it make you feel?"
    - Consequence Questions:
        - "What did that do to your motivation?"
    - High Priority Questions:
        - "Of all that we have covered so far, what is the top priority?"

Practical Exercise: Training in Questioning Skills Instructions

Daily Conversation Improvements (Week 1-2)
- Practice one kind of question regularly within your daily interactions:
- Monday: Raise one clarifying question on each conversation
    - Tuesday: Pose one open-ended question about exploring someone's perspective
    - Wednesday: Preference request: "How do you like?"
    - Thursday: Ask about motives: "What gets you?"
    - Friday: Identify goals: "What would you like to do?"

Weeks 3-4: Goals of Routine
- Perform one deep conversation every week that is entirely focused on growing in question utilization:
    - Select someone you encounter often but do not know very well
    - Prepare 3-4 insightful questions in advance
    - Hear more than you utter

> - Having identified interesting responses, follow up with probing questions
> - Tell what you learned and how it can influence the manner in which your team collaborates

The Appreciative Inquiry Approach

Appreciative Inquiry (AI) is a highly effective approach to involving followers by appealing to strengths, possibilities, and constructive change rather than problems and weaknesses.

Instead of "The thing that is wrong and what can we do about it?" AI poses "The thing that is going right and what can we do about taking advantage of it?"

This approach is practical for understanding and engaging followers because it:
- Creates positive energy and engagement
- Innovates things you never knew you could do
- Builds confidence and encouragement
- Fosters innovative thinking
- Strengthen relationships with positive emphasis

The Four Appreciative Inquiry Stages

- Discovery: Appreciation of What Is
    - In this step, you work with your followers and identify the peak experiences, essential strengths, and points of excellence. You identify the very best of what works.
    - Discovery Questions about Knowledge of Followers:
        - "A moment when you were highly 'alive' and 'in' your work within this institution?"
        - "What do you value most about yourself as a professional?"
        - "Describe a time when you were proud of what you had done."
        - "What about our team makes you do your best work?"
        - "When has our organization been at its best?"
- Dream: Further Than Present Vision
    - The Dream step involves imagining a future where the identified positive traits are developed and enhanced. You are assisting followers in visualizing their ideal work life.
    - Dream Questions:
        - "If you could optimize your perfect workday, what would it entail?"

- "How would our team perform if we were at our very best?"
- "If you had the ability to acquire new skills or take new challenges, what excites you the most?"
- "Picturing our organization three years hence at peak performance. How do you see it?"

- Design: Planning What Should Be
  - In the Design phase, you collaborate and develop solid plans to pursue your dream. This is where understanding solidifies into tangible changes and commitments.
  - Design Activities:
    - Specify what changes would bring the country closer to the dream.
    - Generate new jobs, tasks, or work processes
    - Develop skills and career development strategies
- Destiny: Creating What Will Be
  - The final step involves implementing the designed changes and introducing the appreciative approach to everyday work. It is where knowledge is transferred into long-term involvement.
  - Destiny Actions:
    - Perform implemented improvements and changes

- Track progress and document achievements
- Make appreciative talk a regular practice
- Exhibit and express greatness with other people
- Infuse appreciative inquiry into team culture

Practical Exercise: Workplace Appreciative Inquiry

Apply the following pattern in one-to-one appreciative inquiry interviews with team members:

- Discovery (15 minutes):
    - "I'd love to get what gets your best work out. Describe a particular moment of the past year where you were strongest and most effective in your role?"
    - Follow-up questions:
        - "What made that experience unique?"
        - "What were the circumstances that made it possible for you to succeed?"
        - "What did you discover about yourself from this experience?"
- Dream (15 minutes):
    - "Now I'd like you to imagine the future. You've created your ideal workspace and career. What does it look like?"

- Follow-up questions:
  - "What would you do differently?"
  - "How would you be growing and developing?"
  - "What kind of influence would you have?"
- Design (10 minutes):
  - "Now that we've talked about it, what are 2-3 concrete things we can alter or adopt to go in that direction?"
- Destiny (5 minutes):
  - "What is one thing you'd like to try and uphold within 30 days? How can I help you do so?"

The Trust-Understanding Relationship

When followers believe you truly understand them (their strengths, challenges, motivations, and goals), they're more willing to take risks, share honest feedback, and commit fully to shared objectives.

Trust is built when followers believe:
- Genuine Interest: You are interested because you are curious and not because you are collecting data or fulfilling requirements.
- Follow-Through Consistently: You recall what they say and use it when talking at a later time.

- Adaptive Leadership: You adjust your approach to what you are learning about their needs and interests.

- Confidentiality: They can bring up issues knowing you'll deal with them responsibly.

- Non-Judgmental Listening: You listen to understand, not to judge or criticize.

Constructing Your Follower Knowledge Profile

Develop a comprehensive understanding profile of each team member, beyond common performance data.

Practical Exercise: Follower Comprehension Profile Template

Basic Information
  Name: _____
  Position: _____
  Time with organisation: _____

Preferred Work Styles
  Style of communication (direct/diplomatic, detailed
  Feedback preferences (frequency, method, style): _____
  Decision-making approach (quick/deliberate, independent/collaborative): _____
  Working conditions specifications (work quietly/in groups; structured/varied)

Drivers and Motivations
  Key work drivers: _____
  Short- and long-range career goals:
  _____
  Personal values guiding work:
  _____
  What they find thrilling about their work:
  _____

> **Strengths and Development Areas**
>   Their main strengths when compiling the team: _____
>   Skills they'd like to acquire: _____
>   Where they need assistance: _____
>   How they like to purchase new items: _____
>
> **Relationship Patterns**
>   How they feel about hearing praise: _____
>   How they deal with pressure and stress: _____
>   Why are they confident: _____
>   How they prefer doing work with other people: _____
>
> **Insight and Actions**
>   Core insights regarding leading this individual: _____
>   Actual steps that I will do from this realization: _____
>   How I will refine my leadership style: _____

Encouraging Innovation Through Understanding

When you know your followers intensely, you build psychological safety and tailored encouragement that innovation and creative thinking demand. When individuals feel confident that you comprehend where they are and where they are likely to go, they are more likely to take risks and exchange ideas.

Fostering Conditions of Innovations

- Psychological Safety: They must feel free to take risks, make mistakes, and contribute half-baked ideas without fear of punishment.

- Individual Recognition: Appreciation of personal viewpoints and input makes employees bring their full creativity to work.

- Personalized Support: Innovations are supported differently by different individuals—with resources by some, encouragement by others, and liberty by yet others.

- Learning Orientation: Emphasize what can be learned about failure and success, rather than focusing on the outcome.

Knowing as individuals is valuable, but knowing collectively as a team is of greater value when it comes to leadership effectiveness.

Practical Exercise: Team Dynamics Assessment

Team Interaction Patterns
- Who gets along best?
- Where do communication blunders tend to occur?
- Whose strengths are complemented by team members?
- What are individual persons' contributions within team discourse?

Decision-Making Dynamics
- How does the team usually decide?
- Whose influence is greatest on deciding?
- Is there staff whose work is often undervalued?
- How do team members deal with conflict?

Innovation and Problem-Solving
- Who has the best new ideas?
- How do you reinforce each other when it comes to ideas?
- What kills innovative thinking within team cultures?
- When are the team members at their collaborative best?

Trust and Support Levels

- Which are the strongest relationships on your team?
- Where are the possible breaches of trust?
- How do team members reinforce one another when things go wrong?
- What would boost team cohesion overall?

Action Plan: Fostering Trust
With what you understand about individuals and work groups, create step-by-step action steps to establish trust and engagement:

- Personal Actions (for each team player):
    - One particular manner in which I will demonstrate comprehension of this individual
    - One thing that I will do differently when handling them
    - One opportunity I will create for their growth
    - One way I will adapt my leadership style for them
- Group Activities:
    - One change to improve team communication
    - One initiative to build stronger relationships
    - One process improvement to leverage individual strengths
    - One way to increase psychological safety

Translating Insight into Leadership Application

Getting to understand followers can't possibly be a once-off or annual review discussion. It must become an integral part of your daily leadership approach.

Daily Comprehension Exercises

- Discussion Openers: Initiate conversations using questions related to the person, not just work.
- Active Listening: Pay attention entirely to what others are saying, both verbally and non-verbally.
- Follow-Up Questions: Demonstrate that you recall the earlier conversation by referencing and following up on what has been said.
- Observation: Mark deviations from energy, interest, or performance that may reveal something of interest.

Weekly Comprehension Exercises

- One-on-One Meetings: Devote time to each one-on-one meeting, other than the discussion of the task.
- Team Observation: Observe team interactions and processes to gain insights into individual and group requirements.

- Reflection Time: Reflect on what you learned about your people this week and how it should influence your leadership.

Monthly Understanding Practices

- Deep Conversations: Have at least one deep conversation focused entirely on discovering a team member.
- Pattern Recognition: Integrate pattern detection into what you are reading about individual and team needs.
- Adjusting Your Leadership Style: Align your leadership style by making deliberate adjustments based on increased knowledge.

Wrapping It Up

Engaging and understanding your followers is not a soft skill—but rather a strategic ability that makes possible everything else you do as a leader. When you know what motivates individuals, how they work best, their challenges, and their objectives that drive them forward, you are better positioned to create an environment where they do their very best work.

This understanding also transforms your own leadership practice. Instead of pushing others to perform, you create conditions that motivate individuals to do their best. Instead of leadership by compliance, you lead out of commitment. Instead of pushing harder to get results, you work more smartly by leveraging the individual strengths and motivations of each individual.

The investment you make in understanding your followers yields a performance return on investment, including increased engagement, loyalty, and results. And it makes leadership more rewarding to you and meaningful to those you lead.

Key Takeaways

- Knowing followers is a strategic leadership competence and not just relationship management
- Better questions generate higher understanding and stronger engagement
- Appreciative Inquiry is strength- and possibility-centered, and not problems- and deficit-centered
- Trust is formed when followers are genuinely heard and appreciated
- Appropriate knowledge must go hand in hand with an understanding of team dynamics. Comprehending should become a regular practice of leadership, rather than something done occasionally.

Your Next Steps

- Complete Follower Understanding profiles of each of your team members
- Practice the skills of questioning used in your daily interactions
- Conduct at least one Appreciative Inquiry conversation with a team member.
- Apply the following framework to assess your team dynamics
- Develop and carry out your Trust Building Action Plan
- Make the incorporation of understanding a regular practice of leadership

Questions for Your Team

- In what ways can we improve our understanding and accommodate you in your role?
- How can we better leverage the unique strengths and perspectives of everyone?
- Greater trust and psychological safety within our team would come from: How do we generate greater innovation and inventive thought?

Keep in mind: nobody cares about what you know before they are sure of what you care about. Knowing your followers is where you make good on that care so that it can impact human fulfillment and business results.

Chapter 10

Conversation and Persuasion

You've learned about the fundamentals of communication and understanding your followers.

And now the higher-level skill that separates effective leaders from highly influential leaders: the use of relationship-building conversations that impact results and persuade others to change routes or adopt new concepts.

Every manager believes persuasion is about winning debates or being the most outstanding speaker. Effective influence is a result of your skills in connecting at multiple levels of understanding, recognizing where others are, and steering the conversation toward points of genuine buy-in rather than mere compliance.

This is not manipulation or coercion. This involves learning sophisticated conversation skills that put you in a position to build trust, find common ground, and bring others to acknowledge alternatives they may not have considered. When you are effective at these things, people do not feel coerced—they feel heard and inspired.

> **Reflection Question**
>
> Think about someone who has significantly influenced your thought processing or decision-making. What did they do within discourse that made it possible for you to hear their perspective? How did they listen and make you feel heard and considered while advancing their point of view?

The Three Levels of Leadership Talk

Not all interactions are equally effective. Learning the varying levels of conversation—and knowing when to function at each level—is crucial when it comes to relating and functioning correctly.

First Level: Common Topics and Safe Ground

At this entry level, you are discussing facts, what's currently taking place, and other issues that do not require self-revelation and openness. This is where the majority of work relationships commence and where many stagnate.

Relevant Areas at Level One:
- Market developments and sector trends
- News and current affairs
- weather and travel
- Sport and leisure
- General business presentation
- Uncontroversial global events

The Aim of Level One Conversations:
- Establish basic rapport and comfort
- Find common interests and experiences
- Build a basis for future understanding
- Evaluate preference and style of communication
- Establish first trust with casual interactions

Level One Guidelines:

- Avoid controversial subjects (politics, religion, personal conflicts)
- Seek areas of mutual interest or experience
- Employ this level when analyzing other individuals' ways of communication
- Do not attempt to dash too great a depth

Level Two: Concepts, Views, and Professional Development

This is where relationships are developed on a factual basis. At Level Two, you share viewpoints, discuss tactics, evaluate alternative problem-solving approaches, and openly reveal your thought processes and work values.

Level Two Conversation Topics:
- Strategic management of business problems
- Various views of the industry problems
- Professional growth objectives and interests
- Leadership philosophies and styles
- Innovation and improvement proposals
- Career observations and lessons learned

What Level Two Achieves:
- Exposes how individuals reason and solve problems

- Distinguishes the difference or alignment of approach and values
- Opportunities are developed to impact thinking
- Builds respect based on the interchange of ideas
- Creates mental rapport and mutual respect

Replication at This Level
- State your own views while being truly curious about theirs
- Reasoning questions: "How did you come up with that conclusion?"
- Identify areas of agreement on procedure or values
- Approach respectfully, varying views without seeking points on arguments
- Share experiences that illustrate your points without dominating the conversation

Level Three: Deeper Connections and Personal Experiences

At Level Three, relationships of maximum strength are developed. Here you are sharing personal stories, discussing issues you've encountered, revealing your weaknesses, and building the deep trust that enables true influence and collaboration.

Level Three Components:
- Personal challenges and how you have overcome them
- Failure and what can be learned from it
- Principles that direct your decisions
- Personal or family situations that influenced your outlook
- Fears, Hopes, and Des Key points of change or growth

The Power of Level Three:
- Fosters excellent trust and mutual respect
- Allows openness and tough discussion
- Builds loyalty and commitment
- Permits real influence and persuasion
- Builds long-term career relationships

Level Three Cautions:
- Not always appropriate in all work relationships
- Needs proper discretion of when and what to reveal
- Must be reciprocal—do not reveal if the other is not revealing

- Maintain professional boundaries and remain yourself
- Consider the setting and privacy of your conversation

Practical Exercise: Conversation Level Practice Reference

Weeks 1-2: Achieving Level One Trans
- Daily Practice:
    - Do everything at Level One initially, but don't stick forever
    - Practice noticing 2-3 possible common interests in each conversation
    - Use connecting words: "Speaking of that, I've been thinking about." or "That reminds me of."
    - Complete Level One questions with a question that can bring about Level Two
- Assessment Questions:
    - Am I building comfort and rapport at Level One?
    - Am I effective at recognizing common ground?
    - Am I transitioning legitimately to more advanced material when necessary?

Weeks 3-4: Acquisition of Level Two Skills

- Daily Practice:
    - Discuss one professional viewpoint or experience within each of the main discussions
    - Ask at least one question to gauge the other person's reasoning
    - Practice looking for common ground when you disagree
    - Look for the power of shaping perceptions through ordinary experience
- Quiz Questions:
    - Am I balancing conveying my viewpoints with a genuine interest in others?
    - Do I respectfully explore differences rather than attempt winning arguments?
    - Am I establishing intellectual respect and rapport?

Weeks 5-6: Level Three Discretion and Depth

- Week Exercises:
    - Choose one of your relationships where conversation at Level Three is appropriate
    - Discuss one significant work experience or learning lesson
    - Practice active listening when others share personal insights
    - Notice what more sharing does to the relationship and your influence
- Test Questions:

> - Am I exercising sound judgment regarding when Level Three is proper?
> - Do I maintain professional boundaries and adhere to them?
> - Is greater sharing both a comfortable and mutual experience for both?

Sophisticated Networking: Designing Your Influence Network

Networking is neither about gathering business cards nor about schmoozing at conferences. Strategic networking is about establishing a network of relationships with individuals who can offer insights, opportunities, co-creation of work, and mutual support throughout your career.

Strategic Mindset of Networking

- Value Creation Mindset: Always maintain a context where you can deliver value to others, rather than one where you can receive value from others.

- Long-Term Relationship Formation: Emphasize forming genuine relationships instead of transactional relationships.

- Quality Over Quantity: It is always better if you have a few strong ties rather than a large network of weak ties.
- Mutual Advantage: Good networking connections yield long-term advantages to both individuals.

Networking Conversation Techniques

- The Host/Hostess Approach
    - Host it yourself, even if it is not in your role. Introduce others to one another. Check if others need refreshments. Make others comfortable. This makes you the connector and makes others remember you.
- The Curiosity Strategy
    - Network with genuine interest in others' work, problems, and interests. It is the attention of people of genuine interest that draws others.
- The Value-First Approach
    - Seek places where you can bring value before you request. Include related posts/articles, introductions, insights, or resources that can come in handy.

Practical Exercise: Networking Success Tracker

Pre-Event Planning
- Research attendees and identify 3-5 individuals whom you'd like to connect with
- Prepare 2-3 conversation starters depending on the event
- Set a realistic goal of new relationships (quality, not quantity). Get ready to introduce yourself: position, surname, and something remarkable about your activity.

In-Event Strategy
- Begin with open-ended questions: "Why do you enjoy this performer?"
- Practice the three levels of conversation correctly
- Try to gather other persons of like interest together
- Instead of promoting yourself, try to learn and grow.

Post-Event Follow-Up
- Follow up within 48 hours with tailored communications
- Cite particular points of conversation from your exchange
- Give something of value (article, introduction, resource)
- Indicate a particular next step if applicable

> Monthly Networking Review:
> - Which new relations are taking shape favorably?
> - What did I give up this month within my network?
> - Which networking approaches are working best for me? How can I fortify relationships within my existing network?

Refined Communication Skills: Reading the Room

When grasping the human dynamics at play that underlie all conversation makes the difference between competent and masterful communication. Three higher-level skills can significantly enhance your conversational ability.

Understanding Precipitating Factors

Others bring their entire day, their entire week, with them to every conversation with you. Becoming aware of and considering these precipitating factors permits you to calibrate your manner of communicating and your anticipations to match.

Common Precipitating Factors:
- Stressful mornings (road traffic jams, family problems, computer failure)
- Difficult meetings or discussions earlier in the day

- Competing demands and pressure of work
- Distractions or personal issues
- Physical problems (fatigue, hunger, discomfort
- Recent successful or unsuccessful interactions

Adjusting to Precipitating Factors
- Read the Signs: Note the level of energy, non-verbal bodily cues, and verbal signs.
- Adjust Your M.O.: Tailor your approach according to their state
- Show Empathy: Observe when someone seems stressed or distracted
- Adjust Your Expectations: Don't anticipate full participation if a player is plainly under other pressures
- Offer Flexibility: "Is it a convenient time to talk about this, or do we need to reschedule?"

Finding Common Ground

Common experiences, values, or points of view generate immediate rapport and a basis of influence. Skill is knowing how to find these rapport generators quickly and graciously.

Types of Common Ground

- Common Ground: Similar histories, struggles, or professions
- Common Values: Consensus on what matters at work or in life
- Common Interests: Interests common between industry developments, organisational changes, or problems
- Same Goals: Goal-based aspirations or objectives
- Complementary Views: Varied but harmonious views

Common Ground Conversation Strategies

- "I've had a similar feeling."
- "That reminds me of when I."
- "I believe you when you."
- "Like you, I believe."
- "We both seem to care about."

Using "I" Messages Through Influencing

"It" statements are a valuable tool of communicating feedback, conveying concern, or shaping behavior that do not provoke defensiveness. They are about connecting your experience and what you have observed, and not about imposing judgment or condemnation.

The "I" Message Format:

- Objective Behavior Description: Exactly what happened (fact only)
- Impact Statement: How it affected you or the situation
- Emotional Statement: How you feel (optional but powerful)
- Ask: How would you like things to happen from now on

Example Transformations:

- Rather than: "You are constantly tardy at meetings."
    - When you are absent from the commencement of meetings, I worry that you are not hearing vital information, and the team has wasted their time informing you.
- Rather than: "Your report is sloppy."
    - Experiment: "When I receive reports with varying formatting, I then take additional time editing them before being able to distribute them with top management."
- Rather than: "You never listen to my ideas."

o Try: "When nobody at meetings acknowledges my ideas and I get discouraged about contributing and fear that we are skipping areas where things can be improved."

The Art of Persuasion of the Leader

Persuasion is not about imposing your will on others or winning debates. It is about making other individuals aware of new options, grasping other viewpoints, and deciding to adopt new paths because it is the right thing to do.

The Foundation: Trust and Credibility

You can't convince anyone of anything before you can first ensure that they believe you are
doing what is in their best interest, and that you are qualified to guide them where you are pointing.

Establishing Trust for Persuasion:
- Show genuine interest in their triumph and health
- Discuss your reasoning and decision-making processes candidly
- Admit when you don't know something or when you commit an error
- Show respect for their perspective even when you disagree

Gaining Credibility:
- Refer to relevant experience and knowledge without boastfulness
- Mention specific examples and outcomes of previous situations
- You recognize the difficulty and enormity of what you are proposing
- Show that you have explored some alternatives and perspectives
- Provide evidence and logical reasoning supporting your stance

The Persuasion Procedure

- Step 1: Understand Their Perspective
    - To change someone's mind, you first need to understand their existing stance, concerns, and motivations.
        - How do they feel about it now?
        - Whom do they object to or concern?
        - What would motivate them to do things differently?
        - How do their interests and priorities shift with your proposal?
- Step 2: Identify Common Goals

- Others are easiest to influence when they can grasp how your offer will help them do something they already want.
    - You both are trying to achieve what?
    - Where are your interests converging?
    - How do you put your proposal in terms of mutual goals?
- Step 3: Engage and Respond Actively
    - Manage and overcome objections before they get in the way.
        - "I understand that you are possibly fretting about."
        - "One thing you can't have asked is."
        - "Permit me to speak to what may appear a contradiction."
- Step 4: Argue Your Case
    - Make your appeal of logic, emotion, and evidence strong enough.
        - Use data and information for analytical minds
        - Give examples and stories for those responsive to narrative
        - Appeal based on values and principles toward values-based individuals
        - Stress bottom-line benefits for bottom-line folks
- Step 5: Invite Participation

- Get others to put effort into reframing or translating your proposal. When others put effort toward reframing an idea, they become more invested.
    - "How would you complement this approach?"
    - "How do you suggest we approach its implementation?"
    - "What are you worried about that we need to correct?"

Practical Exercise: Persuasion Skills Test

Self-Assessment Questions (Rate 1-10):
- Trust and Authenticity:
    - People tend to trust my intention and motives: ___/10
    - I acknowledge my mistake and shortcomings honestly: ___/10
    - I arrive on time consistently: ___/10
    - I exhibit expertise without being arrogant: ___/10

- Comprehending Others
    - I try diligently to listen before presenting arguments of mine: ___/10
    - I can properly articulate other people's objections and concerns: ___/10
    - I tailor my persuasion approach based on varying styles of personality: ___/10
    - I recognize common goals and interests correctly: ___/10

- Persuasive Communication
    - I argue rationally and logically: ___/10
    - I use appropriate emotional appeals without manipulation: ___/10
    - I actively and respectfully overcome objections: ___/10

- o Fostering contribution and suggestions toward the solution of problems: ___/10

Scoring Guide:
- 32-40: Effective persuasion skills
- 24-31: Good basis and favorable development prospects
- 16-23: Learning of skills that entail attentional focus
- Below 16: Essential development required

Areas of Development:
- Locate your lowest-scoring sections and work on selective regions of improvement.
- Difficult Conversation Facilitation
- Among the most influential discussions leaders carry on are often the toughest.
- Faced with a structured approach toward uncomfortable discussions raises your confidence and competence when the stakes are at their highest.

Practical Exercise: Difficult Conversation Navigator

To Pre-Conversation Training
- Define Your Purpose:
    - What is the desired endpoint of this discussion?
    - What change or understanding do you need?
    - How will you know if the conversation was successful?

- Anticipate Their Perspective:
    - How would they deal with this issue otherwise?
    - Whose concern or feelings are these?
    - What questions or objections are you likely to have to respond to?

Plan Your Strategy:
- Which of these conversation levels (1, 2, or 3) is used at this topic and relationship level?
- What "I" statements will you use to express your concerns?
- How will you obtain their viewpoint and feedback?

Conversation Structure:

- Introduction (Set the tone and intention): "I'd like to talk about [specific incident]. I intend to listen to your side and work at resolving the matter between both of us."

- Providing Your Opinion (Use "I" Messages): "When [such behavior/situation takes place], I [such effect on you/team/organization], and it makes me feel [your reaction].

- Inviting their perspective: "I'd love to hear what you both think of this issue. How do you both see it?"

Post-Conversation Procedure
- Settle on the agreements reached from the conversation
- Arrange follow-up meetings if necessary
- Track progress toward agreed changes
- Accept changes where you see improvements
- Persuasion Scenarios of Practice: these leaders' common persuasion issues using the models of this chapter

Practical Exercise: Persuasion Scenarios

Scenario 1: Business Processes Modification
- Your team resists change and a new procedure that will increase efficiency, but bring new skills.
- Practice with:
    - Understanding their perspective and concerns
    - Common ground founded on efficiency and achievement
    - Preemptively addressing learning curve problems
    - Inquiring about their views regarding implementation

Scenario 2: Resource Allocation Decisions
- You are
- You are asked to shift funds from one team project account to cover a surprise organisational priority.
- Practice on:
    - Noting the effect on their work
    - Justifying the logic of the selection
    - Finding strategies of resistance against harmful influence
    - Maintaining trust after hearing disappointing news

Scene 3: Performance Requirements
- A top producer has work to do in terms of collaboration with other departments.
- Practice it:
    - Employing "I" statements when describing the effect of existing behavior
    - Linking increased collaboration to career goals
    - Platform-wide collaborative solving of specified enhancements
    - Attaining accountability without micromanaging

Scenario 4: Strategic Direction Change
- The company is changing course and needs your team to acquire new skills.
- Practice using:
    - To make them realize opportunities out of change
    - Overcoming fears about their ability to achieve
    - Preparing a concise development plan
    - Soliciting interest in new work

Wrapping It Up

Learning conversation and persuasion is about far more than being chatty or charismatic. It is about learning the softer interpersonal skills that teach you how to form actual relationships, listen from other perspectives, and move others toward mutually agreed-upon goals with real
influence and not the power of office.

The leaders who are great at these skills don't pressure or intimidate—they connect. They spark discussions where individuals are heard, recognized, and motivated to take action. They establish relationships of trust and credibility where individuals are eager to follow their lead because they believe in the direction the lead is taking them.

They are skills you can learn, but practice and self-reflection are needed. The more you practice these tools consciously in day-to-day interactions, the more effective and spontaneous they become. Begin with the levels of conversation, work on your questioning skills, and then integrate the higher-level persuasion tools based on your feelings of competence.

Key Takeaways

- Different discourse levels are utilized in varying relationships and influence construction tasks.
- Strategic networking is more about mutual value creation than transactional dealings.

- Understanding precipitating factors and common ground enhances all of your communications.
- Persuasion is about being trustworthy, credible, and genuinely concerned about others' interests.
- Difficult conversations can be handled more effectively by using systematic preparation and effective framing. These skills are practiced under conscious practice and observation.

Your Next Steps

- Practice the level of conversation development within your daily interactions.
- Apply the networking strategies at your next work conference
- Use "I" messages when you discuss feedback this week
- Complete the Persuasion Skills Assessment and Determine Areas of Development
- Use the Difficult Conversation Navigator with a complex issue you are experiencing
- Use team persuasion situations with co-workers or mentors

Questions for Your Team

- Which conversation strategies make you relax the most with new ideas or suggestions?
- How can we have more successful debates when we disagree about significant things?
- What would make you feel more comfortable contributing diverse ideas at team meetings?
- How can we improve our ability to trust and believe in each other and other departments?

The craft of great conversation is never about winning an argument; it's about finding the best way forward together. When you inject interest, respect, and co-creating intention into the conversation itself, you are setting the table where influence and desired change can happen.

PART IV: MOTIVATE

Getting the Best from Your People

Chapter 11

Recruiting and Building Your Team

Here is one of those harder-earned realities of leadership: you can't lead your way out of a bad hire. The leadership skills of the first tier are not suddenly going to transform someone of limited ability, character, or cultural fit into someone who can come out and shine within your organization.

So this is when motivation begins, before an individual joins your team—you recruit. It is who you recruit, the manner in which you recruit and bring these individuals into the organization, and how you prepare them for success within the first 90 days of their new role that will decide if your future leadership development is met with high performance or futile frustration.

Everybody treats hiring like it is a necessary evil, something they have to get done fast so they can get on with "real work." Strategic leaders recognize that recruitment and team development are at the top of their list of most important work. Every recruitment decision creates your team's skills, culture, and future for years to come.

This chapter will alter forever the way that you ever think about recruitment—from reactive gap-filling to intentional team building. You'll approach recruitment with the same deliberation that you save for outstanding strategic judgments because recruitment judgments are the very same.

> **Reflection Questions**
>
> Consider your most significant and worst hires. How was your approach, criteria, or process different?
>
> When did you discover the link between team performance and being successful at making hires?

Recruitment as Strategic Leadership

You don't outsource recruitment of HR functions—you can't abdicate this fundamental leadership role; it has a direct bearing on whether or not you can execute your strategic goals. Each recruitment choice fortifies your team's strength at executing your strategy or fills a capability hole you can't cover.

The Strategic Recruitment Mindset

- Future-Oriented Recruitment: Recruit not just for immediate requirements, but recruit for where your organisation is headed. Think about what skills, experiences, and abilities you will require 2-3 years downstream.

- Culture Building: Every hire either reinforces or dilutes your desired culture. Be intentional about the values, behaviors, and attitudes you're adding to your team.

- Teams' Composition: Consider what one individual recruit has that is not yet found within a team. Where are skill gaps in perspective or work styles?

- Competitive Advantage: You can achieve a competitive advantage with one successful recruitment. One failed recruitment can eliminate all your strengths.

Three Types of Recruitment Needs

Knowing why you are hiring makes it easier to hire more strategically and prepare new employees for success.

- Unexpected Departures
    - When someone leaves suddenly due to resignation, termination, illness, or personal circumstances, you're in reactive mode. The key is having recruitment systems ready so you can move quickly without compromising quality.
    - Strategic approach:
        - Make regular contact with likely candidates
        - Resume job duties and requirements
        - Prepare assessment processes available for immediate use
        - Do consider promotion from within first
- Expected Develop
    - Retirements, promotions, transfers, and seasonal needs can be planned in advance, allowing for thorough recruitment and smooth transitions.
    - Strategic approach:
        - Start recruitment 3-6 months before the projected requirement
        - Develop succession planning for main posts
        - Overlap times when departing and arriving persons can mingle

- - - Employ the transition period for thorough onboarding
- Strategic Expansion
  - Adding jobs to cover growth, new projects, or changed strategic imperatives gives you maximum freedom to select and be strategic.
  - Strategic approach:
    - Specify exactly how this role is supporting your strategic goals
    - Evaluate developing internal expertise against bringing in outside talent
    - Budget the complete cost of bringing on a team member (payroll cost, benefits, training facility space)
    - Specify the success criteria of the new role impact

Practical Exercise: Recruitment Planning Template

Position Analysis:

    Job Title: _____
    Department: _____
    Reports to: _____

Type of Recruitment: Unanticipated / Anticipated / Strategic Expansion

Target End Date: _____

Strategic Alignment:
- How does this role contribute at the strategic level? _____
- What specific outcomes must this person achieve in their first year? _____
- How will this function evolve and grow with our strategies? _____

Team Fit Analysis:
- Which team capabilities will this role fill that are currently a hole? _____

- Which of the following working styles or attitudes would suit our team?

  _____

- Which of these cultural features are crucial to this role?

Success Indicators:
- 30-Day Success Indicators:

  _____

- 90-day performance measurements:

  _____

- Annual performance Indicators:

  _____

Sourcing Candidates: Creating Your Talent Pipeline

Waiting until a spot becomes available before starting your candidate search puts you at a tangible disadvantage. Star candidates are rarely actively looking—the best candidates are excelling where they are and only consider a move when presented with something solid.

Builds Ongoing Talent Connections

- Industry Networking: Maintain contacts with industry high achievers, regardless of whether you are actively hiring. Attend conferences, join professional associations, and participate in industry events.
- Internal Referrals: Good employees are usually acquainted with other great professionals. Implement referral programs that compensate employees for referring top candidates.
- University Relations: For positions that require innovative thinking or specialized skills, cultivate relationships with relevant academic departments and career centers.
- Professional Groups: Engage with online communities, industry groups, and forums where your preferred likely candidates are likely to post.

Multi-Channel Purchasing Strategy

- Direct Outreach: Try to find individuals with that particular experience and conduct interviews with them, whether they are actively pursuing jobs.
- Career Networks: Tap into LinkedIn, sector-specific employment boards, and sector

associations to find and connect with talented candidates.

- Employment Referrals: Systematically canvass and discover what your employees know of persons who can fill the positions you are trying to fill.
- Employment Partners: When dealing with specialized or senior roles, utilize employment partners who understand your industry and culture.
- Content Marketing: Develop content that positions your organization as a preferred choice for work and entices passive candidates by highlighting your culture and job opportunities.

Learning the Selection Procedure

The decision-making process is where you transition from identifying possible candidates to selecting the individual who will work with you. This is where you need a systematic procedure that considers both ability and suitability with fairness and legality.

Job Analysis and Needs Definition

You can't possibly select the right person if you are not crystal clear about what the role entails and what success looks like.

Core Requirements:
- Essential skills and experience you can't do without
- Key knowledge and certifications
- Minimum education or experience requirements
- Key skills for being successful within this particular position

Preferred qualifications:
- Additional skills that are useful but not mandatory
- Experience that would have reduced ramp-up time
- Skills that would increase with the role
- Attributes that would enhance teamwork

Cultural and Behavioral Match:
- Match of values with organisational culture
- Integrative work styles of the team
- Communication and collaboration strategies

- Flexibility and learning orientation

The Selection Process Model

Application Screening (20% of time invested)
- Sort resumes and applications against the listed requirements
- Search for evidence of ability and of appropriate experience
- Look for unambiguous disqualifiers or red flags
- Shortlist candidates for first interviews

Initial Interviews (30% of time spent)
- Define key qualifications and interest level.
- Assess the ability to communicate and cultural fit
- Discuss motivation and career goals
- Indicate candidates for extended testing

Comprehensive Test (40% of time spent)
- In-depth interviews with several team members
- Skills assessment or work samples, if necessary
- Background checks with previous co-employees and bosses,

- Evaluation of cultural fit via diversified interactions

Ultimate Decision (10% of the time spent)
- Pair the best candidates with complete qualifications
- Verify final sources and conduct background checks
- Extend the offer of employment with terms and conditions defined
- Confirm acceptance and get ready for onboarding

Interview Questioning Techniques

The interview questions that you employ dictate what data you gather, and what data you gather dictates the validity of your work choices. There are different question styles used for various purposes, including understanding candidates.

Behavioral Interview Questions

Behavioral questions probe what candidates did in the past under certain circumstances, based on the ideology that past behavior is the best indicator of future performance.

Format: "Tell me about a time when." or "Describe a situation where."

Example Questions by Competency:
- Influence and Leadership:
    - "Determine a context where you had to persuade someone to adopt a mindset that they initially resisted."
    - "Tell me about an experience where you led a group of people through the midst of significant change.
- Problem-Solving and Decision-Making
    - "Walking me through a complex issue you've overcome and your methodology."
    - "Describe a time when you had to make a big decision based on limited information."
- Cooperation and Communication:
    - "Tell about a time when you had to collaborate with someone whose manner of speaking was very different from yours."
    - "Cite an instance when you had to give tough feedback to someone you work with."
- Learning and Flexibility:

- "A moment when you had to quickly learn something new and use it to succeed at work?"
- "Describe a situation when priorities were suddenly changed midstream on a project."

Situational Interview Questions

Situational questions are hypothetical scenarios relevant to the role, prompting candidates to describe how they would approach them. They are instrumental in gauging approach and judgment when candidates lack actual experience with similar situations.

Format: "What would you do if..." or "How would you handle."

Example Situation Questions:
- "What would you do if you found that one of the team members was not fulfilling their obligations but was popular with all others?"
- "How would you manage your first 90 days at the office when you were hired?"
- "How would you handle it if you were disagreeing with a top management choice and it was impacting your team?"

Technical and Competency Questions

In positions needing particular skills or technical knowledge, put questions that test these abilities right on.

Technical Skills Test:
- Ask candidates to describe concepts or work role processes
- Provide them with actual problems like what they'd encounter at work
- Ask about work samples or portfolio review when necessary
- Mention functional exercises or a brief presentation

Practical Activity: Interview Question Bank

Behavioral Questions - Leadership Competency:
- Initiative and Enterprise:
    - "Tell about a situation when you recognized a point of improvement being overlooked by other individuals."
- Team Building:
    - "How do you deal with relationships with new team members?"
    - Performance management:
    - "Walking me through the steps of how you supported a struggling staff member in improving."

Situational Questions - Role-Based
- For Managerial Roles:
    - "If you were inheriting a team with low morale and low performance, what would you do within the first 90 days?"

- For Individual Contributor Roles:
    - "How would you manage work priorities if you received conflicting deadlines from diverse stakeholders?"
- In Sales Roles:

> - "How would you react if a client became angry about something within your control?"
>
> Cultural Fit Questions:
> - Value Alignment:
>   - "Describe a work environment where you were very productive and happy. Why was it effective?"
> - Working Approach:
>   - "How do you like to give and receive feedback, and what do you like to be complimented about?"
> - Growth Mindset
>   - "Teach me about a mistake you made early in your career and what you learned from it."

Not Discriminating During Selection

Unconscious bias can provoke employment decisions based on irrelevant instead of performance-based criteria, and deserving candidates of varying backgrounds are overlooked. It is preferable both for fairness and recruitment quality if deliberate mechanisms of suppressing bias are implemented.

Common Forms of Employment Bias

- Confirmation Bias: Seeking information that supports our initial impression instead of critically analyzing all available evidence.

- Affinity Bias: Preference for those candidates with a similar background, interests, or experience to our own.

- Halo Effect: Allowing one individual's strong positive feature to dominate other strong features.

- Recency Effect: Being overly influenced by the most recent interviews when making final decisions.

- Attribution Bias: Making assumptions about why someone succeeded or failed at earlier jobs and never knowing the full context.

Practical Activity: Checklist of Bias Identification

Pre-Interview Planning
- Establish clear, task-focused criteria prior to making any choice
- Common interview questions applicable to all candidates
- Utilizing several interviewers to obtain varying perspectives
- Scoring system based on specified competencies

During Interviews:
- Asked the same fundamental questions of each candidate
- Wrote careful notes rather than relying on memory
- Concentrated on individual illustrations and evidence, and not on impressions
- Avoided personal topics unrelated to job performance

Post-Interview Assessment
- Assessed each applicant on pre-defined specifications
- Compared candidates with the needs of the job, not with each other

- Faced all evidence equally, both memorable and other
- Involved quite a few persons when making the final decision

Red Flags to Watch Out for:
- Making hasty resolutions within the first few minutes
- Feeling strangely elated or distraught with no apparent reason
- Embracing more of a cultural orientation rather than cultural alignment
- Overcredentialing of qualifications versus actual competence
- Rationalizing based on no evidence

Structured Decision-Making Process

- Individual Assessment: Each interviewer shall individually assess candidates based on pre-specified criteria and then deliberate collectively as a group.
- Evidence-Based Conversation: Support arguments with concrete illustrations and data instead of gut feelings or sentiments.

- Devil's Advocate: Get somebody to play devil's advocate so you can anticipate possible objections.
- Reference Check Confirmation: Utilize reference discussions to confirm or dispel perceptions formed during interviews.

Background Check and Making Offers

Thorough final steps before making a final offer are verification of the information candidates have provided and ensuring they are the right fit within your organization.

Thorough Background Check

- Employment Record: Check dates, titles, and overall duties with former employers. Emphasize evaluating performance and work quality when available.
- Credentials: Ensure that degrees, certifications, and professional licenses are valid and up-to-date.
- Reference Letters: Speak individually with former bosses and coworkers who can provide information about your work ability and personality.
- Skills Verification: Practical examinations or the performance of portfolios can be utilized for verifying the skills alleged.

- Compliance with Law: Ensure that all background checks are conducted in accordance with local, state, and federal statutes regarding what information can and cannot be legally obtained.

Making Good Offers

A job offer is more than about pay—it is the first instant you can converse and inspire your recruit.

- Component Ingredients:
  - Base pay and variable pay
  - Benefits package and perks
  - Career development prospects
  - Prospects of growth and career development
  - Work arrangement flexibility
  - Commencement date and any transition aid

- Presentation Approach:
  - Hand-deliver to individuals, rather than using HR when possible
  - Talk about how the role is advancing your team's strategic goals
  - Spotlight specific growth and influence chances
  - Replying to whatever questions or problems they raised when conducting interviews

- o Allow sufficient time to deliberate when setting clear deadlines.

Onboarding for Success

The first 90 days determine whether the new hire will be a long-term performer or a costly error. Systematic onboarding prepares individuals to succeed and gets them up to speed faster on your team's goals.

Strategic Framework of Onboarding

Pre-Day One Preparation:
- Workspace available, equipment and system access ready
- Welcome items and team introductions timed
- First-week schedule made with a blend of orientation and practical work
- Mentor or buddy designated for informal support

Week One: Foundation Setting
- Personal welcome and team introductions
- Detailed role prescriptions and yardsticks for gauging success
- Overview of team performance and work relationships

- First work that instills confidence and value added

Month One: Integration
- Frequent check-ins to cover questions and issues
- Greater autonomy and accountability
- Early performance and cultural fit information
- Introduction of key partners and supporters

Month Two: Contribution
- Full participation with team work and projects
- Peer relationships growing spontaneously
- Independence from all other daily activities
- Contributing ideas and information toward team goals

Month Three: Optimization
- Performance appraisal and alignment with objectives
- Determination of development prospects
- Determine
- Long-term inclusion in team cultures
- Planning for the future growth and development.

Practical Exercise: Onboarding Checklist

Pre-Arrival Preparation:
- Workspace is ready with adequate equipment and supplies
- Testing of access provisioning to IT systems
- Customized welcome folder with essential details
- First-day schedule created and shared
- Team made aware of the new recruit's background and commencement date

Day One:
- Direct Supervisor Personal Welcome
- Facilities tour and orientation of the immediate team
- Verification of performance measures and role assumptions
- Completion of system installation and training
- Meal with team or influential colleagues

Week One Objectives:
- Complete requisite compliance and HR training
- Introduce all team members and key stakeholders

- Know team goals and immediate priorities
- Finish the first significant work project
- Regular check-ins with a supervisor

30-Day Milestones
- Self-sufficient in basic work responsibilities
- Comfortable with team processes and communications
- Introducing ideas and perceptions to teamwork
- Fostering successful relationships with co-workers
- Clear understanding of performance requirements

60-Day Review:
- Official comment and performance appraisal session
- Career development discussion and planning
- Evaluation of team fitness and related fine-tuning
- Additional growth objective establishment
- Initiating greater autonomy and initiative

90-Day Integration:

- Active team member toward team goals and values
- Peer relationships were formed and were successful
- Attaining or surpassing the requirements of performance
- Plan of long-term development adopted
- Celebration of successful integration

Long-Term Retention Plan

It makes sense to hire competent workers only if their interests and performance are sustained at high rates over time. Retention is not only initiated at recruitment and onboarding but is extended beyond repeated development, engagement, and career growth.

Understanding Retention Drivers

- Meaningful Work: Employees remain when their work is meaningful and has a connection with their values and interests.
- Growth Opportunities: High achievers require a clear career path for future development,

grounded in opportunities for promotion, additional responsibilities, or skill enhancement.

- High-Quality Relationships: Good relationships with bosses and colleagues are perhaps one of the strongest predictors of employee engagement and retention.

- Appreciation and Recognition: Timely appreciation of effort and work cements the value individuals bring to the firm.

- Compensation and Benefits: Competitively reasonable and fair overall rewards help reduce the likelihood that individuals will price shop elsewhere due to financial considerations.

- Blurring of Work and Family: Flexibility and work-family accommodation increase commitment and decrease burnout.

Practical Activity: Retention Strategy Worksheet Instructions

Individual Retention Planning:
- In evaluating each team player:
    - Employer Name: _____
    - Engagement Level: High / Medium / Low
    - Risk of Flight: Low / Medium / High
- Central Drivers
    - What propels this individual toward their best work?
- Career Aspirations
    - Where do they envision themselves in 2-3 years?
- Development Needs:
    - Which skills or experiences would move their goals forward?
- Relationship Quality:
    - How strong is their identification with their team and firm?
- Retention Strategies:
    - Specific steps towards increased engagement and retention:

Company-Wide Retention Strategies
- Regular career development conversations

- Skill development chances based on a person's targets
- Milestone awards that honor various forms of contributions
- Compressed work arrangements that suit work-life blending
- Clear paths of advancement and promotion requirements
- Competitive pay reviews and changes
- Team-building activities that strengthen relationships

Cultivating a Retention-Based Culture
- Stay Conversations: Regular chats about what is and is not functioning and where things can work better before things become reasons for leaving.

- Growth Planning: An Organized procedure of specifying each person's career aspirations and extracting development steps toward them.

- Feedback Climate: A place where individuals are constantly provided with feedback on their performance and are allowed chances to impact their work setting.

- Autonomy and Trust: Granting employees control of their work processes and alternatives, and being only responsible for results.

Wrapping It Up

Leading a high-performance team is based on effective recruitment and deliberate onboarding. Each recruitment choice enhances your team's ability to do what you are trying to accomplish or creates difficulties that will inhibit your ability to lead.

Upfront investment made in effective recruitment, selective selection, and effective onboarding gets returned years later in performance, engagement, and retention. When you recruit strategically and place candidates in a position to perform on day one, it makes life easier as a leader because you are working with individuals with the ability, cultural alignment, and momentum to succeed.

The alternative—reactive hiring, poor onboarding, and high turnover—creates a cycle of constant recruitment, training, and performance management that prevents you from focusing on strategic leadership priorities. Make recruitment and team building the strategic priority they ought to be. All of your future leadership is hanging in the strength of the team you recruit and develop now.

Key Points

- Recruitment is a strategic leadership role and not an administrative task
- Knowing what you are hiring for allows you to recruit better and get expectations right
- Systematic choice reduces prejudices and enhances recruitment quality
- The first 90 days determine the long-run survival of new team members
- Retention strategies must come early at recruitment and remain constant throughout employment relationships
- Every recruitment choice determines the team's culture and capacity for years

Your Next Steps:

- Fill out the Recruitment Planning Template for any existing or future recruitment requirements

- Derive role-specific interview questions from the available frameworks
- Use the Bias Recognition Checklist at your next recruitment session
- Develop detailed onboarding checklists based on diverse role classifications
- Evaluate retention risks and chances with existing team members
- Make regular talent pipeline connections before you have jobs available to fill

Questions for Your Team

- In what ways can our team get stronger in terms of skills, perspectives, or capability?
- How can we enhance our onboarding system to enable new employees to achieve higher rates of success?
- Which retention factor is of most significant concern to you at the moment within your career?
- How can we strengthen our employer brand to attract the skills we need?

Keep in mind: You can't motivate your way out of a bad hire, but you can hire your way into making things easier to motivate. Spend the time and effort it takes to get the right team, and everything else gets easier.

www.ingramcontent.com/pod-product-compliance
Lightning Source LLC
Chambersburg PA
CBHW020453030426
42337CB00011B/95